drink
to your health

ANITA HIRSCH, M.S., R.D., has worked in the food and nutrition field for almost thirty years – more than twenty of them spent developing and testing recipes for health books and magazines. She is a college teacher and a regular health-food columnist on several U.S. newspapers. She lives in Pennsylvania.

drink
to your health

Anita Hirsch, M.S., R.D.

Delicious, Easy-to-Prepare
Juices, Smoothies,
Teas, Soups,
and Other Beverages
That Deliver
Vitality and
Immunity

BANTAM BOOKS

LONDON · NEW YORK · TORONTO · SYDNEY · AUCKLAND

DRINK TO YOUR HEALTH
A BANTAM BOOK : 0 553 81412 5

First publication in Great Britain

PRINTING HISTORY
Bantam edition published 2002

1 3 5 7 9 10 8 6 4 2

The material in this book is not meant to take the place of diagnosis
and treatment by a qualified medical practitioner. Any
recommendation set forth in the following pages is undertaken
at the reader's sole risk. The author and publishers disclaim
any liability arising directly or indirectly from the use of this book.

Set in Centaur, FranklinGothic and Seagull by
Phoenix Typesetting, Ilkley, West Yorkshire.

Bantam Books are published by Transworld Publishers,
61–63 Uxbridge Road, London W5 5SA,
a division of The Random House Group Ltd,
in Australia by Random House Australia (Pty) Ltd,
20 Alfred Street, Milsons Point, Sydney, NSW 2061, Australia,
in New Zealand by Random House New Zealand Ltd,
18 Poland Road, Glenfield, Auckland 10, New Zealand
and in South Africa by Random House (Pty) Ltd,
Endulini, 5a Jubilee Road, Parktown 2193, South Africa.

Printed and bound in Great Britain by
Cox & Wyman Ltd, Reading, Berkshire.

This book is dedicated with thanks to my mom, Mildred Sher, who taught me to eat with health in mind, to cook with love for those you love, to recycle leftovers, and be delighted with a fresh peach for dessert.

Contents

contents

contents

5   soups, broths, and hot beverages   141

6   milks   173

contents

contents

Thank you to my always-patient husband, Sy, who suggested the title, and who tasted and critiqued all of my experiments. (I told Sy to expect a beverage for every meal including breakfast. He said 'I've tasted my first glass of toast.') Thank you to my daughter Leanne, who called whenever she found something that I should include, and to my son, Michael, who kept me abreast of the latest food trends.

Thank you to my colleague, Jane Zeigler M.S., R.D., C.N.S.D., assistant professor and director for the Allen Center For Nutrition at Cedar Crest College in Allentown, Pennsylvania, who reviewed my manuscript. Thank you to Deborah Gore, R.D., who guided me down realistic and practical nutritional paths. Thank you to Marian Wolbers and Brenda Bortz, who lovingly shared their creativity and energy. Thanks both to my agent Ellen Greene and to my editor Matthew Lore. Thanks also to Pauline Neuwirth for a terrific book design, Susi Oberhelman for a beautiful cover, and Eileen DeWald for marshalling the manuscript through production.

A huge thank you to Diana Delling, the editor who whipped the manuscript into shape.

ESHA Research, Inc., The Food Processor, was used to analyse the recipes for nutrition content.

Introduction

You may have heard that tea helps prevent heart disease and cancer. You may have heard that cranberry juice can prevent or cure urinary tract infections. You may have even heard that soya milk fights cancer and may help to ease the symptoms of menopause.

Well, all of these things are true. And as you'll learn by reading and using this book, beverages can deliver many other powerful health benefits — and taste great, too.

The beverages in this book promote vitality and immunity. Some of them will lift your spirits when you're down in the dumps, while some will help your body fight off a cold or flu. Some of these drinks will energize you, some will help you relax after a long day at work. If you suffer from a chronic illness, you'll find something in this book that may help you achieve optimal health. And if you're worried about getting enough vitamins and minerals in your daily diet, there's a drink in this book that can help you, too.*

the choice is yours

After twenty-eight years in the food and nutrition field (twenty-two of them spent developing and testing recipes for health books and magazines), I have some strong opinions about a healthy diet. You need to choose foods that will benefit your health. Don't pick foods simply because you are hungry for them, because they will fill you up, or because they are convenient. And don't eat strawberry shortcake when plain strawberries will do.

Unfortunately, when it comes to beverages, many of us seem to be making choices that are quick and convenient rather than healthy. In the U.S. milk consumption is down, while soft drink consumption continues to rise. Sugars and other sweeteners, coming mostly from soft drinks, currently account for 20 per cent of the calories in the average American teenager's diet. In 1994, the average teenager drank 64.5 gallons of soft drinks each year, up from 20.6 gallons in 1978!

Many of the popular new bottled coffee and tea drinks are brimming with sugar. If you check the labels carefully, you'll see that one bottle of sweetened ice tea contains 2.5 servings, or more than 200 calories, and provides hardly any vitamins or minerals.

Even the 'juice' drinks we buy for our children (and for ourselves) are suspect. Too often they are little more than water, high fructose corn syrup, artificial flavours and colourings, and preservatives. Most contain less than 2 per cent real juice!

But there *are* alternatives. A fresh fruit drink prepared from a recipe in this book (Mango Milk, for example) may cost about 70p per serving — a little more than a commercial juice drink, perhaps, but you're getting so much more nutrition for your money. The delicious fresh fruit drinks and smoothies in this book are naturally sweet and colourful (your kids will love them). They provide our bodies with important vitamins, dietary fibre, and lots of healing phytochemicals. And they *don't* contain high-fructose corn syrup.

quick meals for those on the go

In these fast-paced times, it can be hard to find time for a full sit-down meal. A healthy beverage, carried in a mug or thermos, makes a wonderful, nutritious meal on the go. Beverages should not substitute for every meal; sitting down to eat a meal with others can be healing in itself. But a healthy drink is certainly a better choice than a vending-

machine selection or a greasy fast-food meal. Nutrient-dense drinks
– those that provide lots of nutrients for every calorie they contain –
make excellent meal replacements. (Try the Morning Superstart when
you don't have time for breakfast.) Even the soups I've included in this
book can be puréed and sipped on the road.

make beverages
part of your healthy diet

Juice drinks, smoothies, and puréed soup beverages are great ways to
add fruits and vegetables to your daily diet. The National Cancer
Society recommends at least five servings a day of fruits and vegetables
for optimum health; I've heard other experts advocate up to 10 servings of fruit and vegetables a day, including one high-vitamin C fruit
or vegetable at every meal.

Healthy beverages are also delicious ways to provide your body with
vitamins, minerals, and nutrients you wouldn't otherwise be getting in
your daily diet. A cup of tasty Doubly Green Tea provides a hefty dose
of immune-strengthening vitamin C, for example. And one serving of
the Hi-Po smoothie supplies almost half the day's requirement of
potassium.

Each recipe in this book is followed by a nutrition analysis that
provides information on the calories, protein, carbohydrates, fat,
cholesterol, dietary fibre, and sodium contained in each serving. Most
of the recipes are low in fat (less than 5 grams per serving), low in
sodium (less than 300mg), and high in dietary fibre (3g or more). If
you wish to reduce your intake of refined sugar, feel free to substitute
a non-calorific sweetener when sugar is called for.

The analysis also notes which vitamins and minerals are abundant
in each drink. Drinks labelled 'high in' a nutrient contain at least
20 per cent of the recommended Daily Value of that nutrient.
Drinks labelled 'a good source of' a nutrient contain between 10 and
20 per cent of the recommended Daily Value of that nutrient.
Look for beverages with flavours that appeal, the nutrients you need,
or both!

medicinal drinks

Do you have a specific health problem or concern? There may be a beverage that can help prevent that disease or provide relief from your symptoms. Herbal teas have medicinal properties – echinacea tea, for example, can strengthen the immune system and help shorten the duration of a cold. And certain foods contain nutrients that make them beneficial for persons with specific medical conditions. Foods that are rich in calcium, magnesium, and potassium, for example, can actually help control high blood pressure. For information on which beverages are recommended to treat or prevent specific health conditions, consult the Ailments Index on p.215.

don't forget the water

I encourage you to try as many of the recipes in this book as you can. But I also urge you to remember the most important healthy beverage of all: water. Our need for water is second only to our need for oxygen. Water makes up more than half of our body weight and is a necessary component of all our vital body fluids: blood, the digestive juices, urine, and perspiration. Water plays a crucial role in every one of our bodily functions and transports nutrients throughout our bodies.

Drink at least 8 glasses of clear, fresh water – 1.120 l – a day. Carry it with you in a bottle or thermos, or keep it in the refrigerator at home and at work. Leave a water bottle or glass in full view on your desk; it will serve as a reminder to drink more water.

drink to your health

Drink to Your Health is filled with more than 125 delicious, fast, and easy to prepare beverages. These drinks are made using healthy ingredients that are available in your local supermarket or health food shop. They are naturally sweet or require minimal amounts of added sweeteners. And none of them rely on artificial flavours or colours for their great taste.

A cooker or microwave and an immersion or regular blender or a food processor are all the equipment you'll need to prepare the beverages in this book. (Sometimes little more than a long-handled iced-tea spoon or a simple hand-held whisk will do.) An electric juicer is required in a few of the recipes, but because juicing removes most of the dietary fibre from a fruit or vegetable, I've kept juicer-processed drinks to a minimum. Most of the juices and smoothies included here are made by puréeing fruits and vegetables in a blender, which preserves their valuable fibre content. To prepare these blender drinks or smoothies when on the go, you can purchase a blender that plugs into a vehicle's cigarette lighter.

I hope you find that these delicious drinks make an important contribution to your good health, and that *Drink to Your Health* becomes a trusted and important addition to your library of cookbooks.

* All references to Recommended Daily Value equals Recommended Daily Allowance.

1

Cool, refreshing juice drinks combine sweet fruit and vegetable juices to create beverages with exciting new flavours and optimal nutritional benefits. Generally high in vitamins A and C, juice drinks are excellent immune system strengtheners.

juices
plain and fancy

Arthritis Relief

Fresh strawberry and pineapple juices make this refreshing drink high in vitamin C, an antioxidant thought to be particularly beneficial for those with rheumatoid arthritis. Vitamin C promotes collagen production and the repair of connective tissue. Those who take aspirin for pain relief should be sure to include extra vitamin C in their diets because aspirin depletes the body's natural supply.

> 125 ml fresh strawberry juice (8 to 10 strawberries)
> 125 ml fresh pineapple juice (about 438 g pineapple chunks)
> ⅛ teaspoon sugar (optional)
> ice

Combine the ingredients, add ice, and enjoy.

yield:

1 serving (250 ml)

per serving:

106 calories, 1 g protein, 26 g carbohydrates, 0.5 g total fat, 0 mg cholesterol, 0 g dietary fibre, 3 mg sodium. High in vitamin C. A good source of vitamin B⁶, folate, and potassium.

Cancer Phyter

Tangy, nutrient-packed Cancer Phyter is high in sulforaphane glucosinolate (sulforaphane GS), an antioxidant and phytochemical found in cruciferous vegetables that stimulates the body's immune system and may help reduce the risk of some types of cancer. It's made with BroccoSprouts, a nutritional broccoli sprout developed by the Johns Hopkins University Medical Center. A one-ounce serving of BroccoSprouts contains as much sulforaphane GS as 3 ounces of cooked broccoli — so a little of this drink goes a long way.

If BroccoSprouts aren't available, use fresh broccoli instead. You'll get a slightly sweeter beverage, but you'll need to drink more to get your dose of sulforaphane GS.

> 25 g BroccoSprouts, rinsed, or 1 stalk raw broccoli, rinsed
>   and trimmed
> 125 ml carrot juice (5 or 6 carrots)
> ½ clove garlic
> 1 teaspoon chopped onion

Combine the ingredients in the juicer and juice. For a less tangy taste, add more carrots. Serve.

yield:
>   1 serving (25 g if using sprouts; 50 g if using broccoli)

per 125 ml serving with sprouts (estimated):
>   38 calories, 2 g protein, 8 g carbohydrates, 0.2 g fat, 0 mg cholesterol, 0 mg dietary fibre, 62 mg sodium. High in vitamin A, vitamin C, and beta carotene.

phytochemicals

Phytochemicals, or plant chemicals, are substances found in fruits and vegetables that scientists believe can prevent disease in humans and help us maintain healthy immune systems. Further research may shed light on just how and why phytochemicals work in our bodies. While some manufacturers are trying to isolate them in pill form, eating a variety of fruits and vegetables is the best way to make sure that phytochemicals are included in your diet.

phytochemical	food
Allium	onions, garlic, spring onions, leeks, chives
Caffeic Acid	fruits
Carotenoids:	
alpha and beta carotene	orange vegetables and fruits
lutein	green leafy vegetables
lycopene	tomatoes, red grapefruit, guava, watermelon
cryptoxanthin	tangerines, papaya, oranges, mango, peaches, nectarines
Coumarins	citrus fruits, parsley, carrots
Dithiolthiones	cruciferous vegetables: kale, broccoli, cauliflower, Brussels sprouts, cabbage, bok choy, greens, swede, turnips
Ellagic Acid	grapes, blueberries
Ferulic Acid	fruits
Flavonoids:	
Quercetin	tea, wine, apples, onions, celery
Kaempferol	cranberries, grapes, broccoli, endive
Indole-3 carbinol	cruciferous vegetables

Isoflavones:
    Genistein   soya beans, kidney beans, chickpeas, lentils

Isothiocyanates:
    sulphoraphane   cruciferous vegetables

Lignans   flaxseed

Limonene   citrus fruits

Phytic Acid   grains

Phytosterols   soya beans and dried beans

Protease inhibitors   soya beans and dried beans

Saponins   soya beans and dried beans

Tutti Fruiti on the Rocks

Prune juice is the old stand-by when it comes to constipation relief, but not everyone likes its taste. This drink combines prune juice with apricot purée to improve its flavour and add the benefits of vitamin C and beta carotene. Tutti Fruiti makes a good breakfast drink. Try one every morning to promote regularity.

> 125 ml apricot purée
> 125 ml prune juice
> ice

Combine and serve over ice.

yield:
1 serving (250 ml)

per serving:
161 calories, 1 g protein, 41 g carbohydrates, 0.2 g fat, 0 mg cholesterol, 2 g dietary fibre, 9 mg sodium. High in vitamin A (and beta carotene which is utilized as vitamin A). A good source of carbohydrates, vitamin B[6], vitamin C, iron, and potassium.

Faux Café

Allentown, Pennsylvania, registered nurse Marie Melick finds that warm prune juice does the trick for her patients with constipation. Served with a touch of milk, a cup of Faux Café in the morning should bring relief.

> 125 ml prune juice
> 2 tablespoons skimmed milk

Warm prune juice in a mug in the microwave or in a small saucepan on the cooker. Add the milk and serve warm.

yield:

1 serving (125 ml)

per serving:

104 calories, 2 g protein, 24 g carbohydrates, 0.4 g fat, 1 mg cholesterol, 1 g dietary fibre, 21 mg sodium. A good source of vitamin B^6 and potassium.

High-C

A terrific boost for the body's immune system, High-C contains 73 mg of vitamin C – more than 100 per cent of the recommended Daily Value. Tomatoes supply additional cancer- and disease-fighting nutrients.

½ tomato, skinned
125 ml orange juice
1 teaspoon lemon juice
1 teaspoon honey

Combine ingredients in blender and process until smooth.

yield:
1 serving (250 ml)

per serving:
104 calories, 2 g protein, 23 g carbohydrates, 0.3 g fat, 0 mg cholesterol, 1.3 g dietary fibre, 32 mg sodium. High in vitamin C and folate. A good source of vitamin A, thiamine, iron, and potassium.

choosing
canned tomatoes

Tomatoes are loaded with vitamins A and C and contain the protective phytochemical lycopene. Flavourful, fresh, in-season tomatoes kept at room temperature (not refrigerated) always taste best. But canned tomatoes can be an excellent and convenient substitute. Choose a brand that's low in salt. Canned tomatoes can sometimes taste metallic or salty; those labelled 'fresh cut' or 'fresh flavour' are often good bets. I like Del Monte fresh cut, no-salt-added tomatoes, but do your own taste test and see what you like.

drink to your health

Ginger Apricot Support

Support your good health! Apricots, both fresh and canned, are an excellent source of carotenoids, thought to prevent cancer, heart disease, and stroke. Use bottled apricot purée, or make your own (purée fresh or canned, drained apricots in a blender). Yogurt with active cultures and ginger root give this drink even more nutritional appeal.

> 50 ml plain non-fat yogurt
> 50 ml spring water or mineral water
> 1/8 teaspoon grated ginger root
> 125 ml apricot purée

Combine ingredients in a glass and stir to blend.

yield:
> 1 serving (250 ml)

per serving:
> 105 calories, 4 g protein, 23 g carbohydrates, 0.2 g fat, 1 mg cholesterol, 1 g dietary fibre, 52 mg sodium. High in vitamin A. A good source of calcium.

ginger

Fresh ginger, found in the produce sections of most supermarkets, can help calm an upset stomach, prevent motion
sickness, and stimulate the appetite. It's also good for relieving
migraine headaches.

Choose a piece that is firm and without blue or mouldy spots.
To store, wrap and place the ginger in the produce drawer in the
refrigerator, then use as needed. The skin can be removed or
eaten for added fibre. You can juice fresh ginger by slicing it and
running the slices through a garlic press. Or use a ginger grater.

drink to your health

One-Two Punch

Start with this buttermilk-based beverage – buttermilk is a good source of calcium, which can help prevent osteoporosis. Then follow it up with a little sunshine; the vitamin D that your body makes from exposure to the sun will help deposit the calcium in your bones.

One-Two Punch is particularly recommended for those nursing broken bones. The vitamin C in the pineapple juice helps the body repair bones and generate collagen, which holds the bones together.

> 125 ml pineapple juice, fresh or canned (unsweetened)
> 125 ml buttermilk (low fat)
> 1 teaspoon granulated sugar or mint syrup (see page 204)
> mint leaf (for garnish)

Combine ingredients in a glass and serve. For extra froth, use blender to combine.

yield:
> 1 serving (250 ml)

per serving:
> 136 calories, 5 g protein, 27 g carbohydrates, 1 g fat, 4 mg cholesterol, 0.3 g dietary fibre, 130 mg sodium. High in vitamin C. A good source of calcium, riboflavin, and potassium.

Elizabeth's Healing Cocktail

Elizabeth, who lives in New York City, stops for a healthy beverage every day on the way home from her high-powered job. Her favourite is this combination of raw vegetables – it's high in fibre, antioxidants, and protective phytochemicals.

The sweetness of the carrot and orange juices hides the bitterness of the cabbage juice. If you like, add more carrots to tame its strong flavour. In folk medicine, cabbage and cabbage juice are used to heal ulcers. In one recent study, ulcer patients who drank 1.120 l of cabbage juice daily showed signs of improvement.

- $^1/_8$ small head of cabbage
- 3 carrots
- 1 orange, peeled
- $^1/_4$ small clove garlic (optional)
- $^1/_4$ teaspoon fresh ginger (optional)

Combine ingredients in a juice machine. Juice and serve.

yield:

1 serving (150 ml)

per serving (estimated):

184 calories, 5 g protein, 44 g carbohydrates, 1 g fat, 0 mg cholesterol, 0 g dietary fibre, 96 mg sodium. High in vitamin A, thiamine, niacin, vitamin B[6], vitamin C, folate, calcium, magnesium, potassium. A good source of protein, carbohydrates, riboflavin, vitamin E, pantothenic acid, iron.

cruciferous
vegetables

High-fibre cruciferous vegetables help ward off colon, rectal, and other cancers. Add them to soups, salads, and vegetable juice drinks whenever you can. The family of cruciferous vegetables includes:

Bok choy
Broccoli
Brussels sprouts
Cabbage
Cauliflower
Greens
Kale
Kohlrabi
Mustard greens
Radishes
Rocket
Swede
Turnips
Watercress

Piquant Pomegranate

Fresh pomegranates generally appear in the autumn. We used to buy them and eat them on the way to school. My mother would drop some seeds into a sandwich bag and we would suck the juice out of them. She knew what she was doing – pomegranate juice is high in vitamin C, so the snack provided an immune system boost just at the start of the cold and flu season. This drink will do the same.

125 ml fresh pomegranate juice
250 ml water
2 tablespoons frozen apple juice concentrate
½ teaspoon sugar or fructose or other sweetener

Combine the ingredients in a glass, stir, and serve.

yield:

1 serving (375 ml)

per serving:

115 calories, 0.4 g protein, 29 g carbohydrates, 0 g fat, 0 mg cholesterol, 0 g dietary fibre, 10 mg sodium. A good source of vitamin C and potassium.

juicing
a pomegranate

You can juice a pomegranate in either a juicer or a blender. To juice in a blender, cut the pomegranate in half, scoop out the seeds and the surrounding pulp, and place them in the blender. Turn on the blender for a few seconds – the blender blades will separate out most of the juice. Add a small amount of water and blend for a few more seconds, then pour the juice and seed mixture into a strainer. The juice can be pressed out or strained into a glass. One pomegranate should yield about 125 ml of juice.

Good Time Party Punch

Keep party guests happy *and* healthy with this nutritious punch. Every serving packs 67% of the DV of vitamin C (40 mg), so you can actually encourage them to overindulge. Pineapple juice is also high in potassium and folate (folic acid), which can help prevent heart disease. For extra kick, add fresh ginger juice (see page 32).

500 ml cranberry juice cocktail (see p.121)
500 ml pineapple juice
175 ml ginger syrup (see page 202), 360 ml ginger ale
    (see p.39), or 175 ml fresh ginger juice (see p.32)

Combine and serve. For just one serving, use 75 ml of cranberry cocktail, 75 ml of pineapple juice and 2 tablespoons of ginger syrup, ginger ale, or fresh ginger juice.

yield:
6 servings (about 250 ml each)

per serving:
108 calories, 0.4 g protein, 27 g carbohydrates, 0 g fat, 0 mg cholesterol, 0.3 g dietary fibre, 4 mg sodium. High in vitamin C.

drink to your health

ginger ale

When choosing a commercial ginger ale, check the ingredients label. If it doesn't contain natural ginger, don't bother. Health food shops typically carry natural ginger ales.

You can also make your own ginger ale using ginger syrup (see page 202). This flavourful syrup can be prepared and refrigerated to use for many drinks.

2

Prepared in a blender, smoothies combine frozen or fresh ripe fruits with healthy soya, rice, or dairy milks and yogurts. These thick, colourful drinks deliver phytochemicals and antioxidant vitamins along with protein and lots of flavour.

smoothies and other blender drinks

Nutrient-Dense
Pear-Avocado Abundance

High in fibre and packed with nutrients, this extra-thick beverage makes a healthy snack or meal. Drink it all at once, or divide it up and drink portions throughout the day. With selenium and zinc, it's an excellent flu- and virus-fighter. And because it's high in calcium, magnesium, and potassium, it can also help keep blood pressure under control.

½ avocado, peeled and chunked
½ pear, peeled and chunked
125 ml plain fortified soya milk
50 ml plain non-fat yogurt
50 ml apple juice (more if you prefer a thinner drink)
2 teaspoons wheat germ

Combine all ingredients in blender and process until smooth.

yield:
1 serving (375 ml)

per serving:
366 calories, 13 g protein, 47 g carbohydrates, 17 g fat, 3 g sat fat, 8 g mono fat, 1 mg cholesterol, 11 g dietary fibre, 109 mg sodium. High in protein, beta carotene, vitamin A, vitamin C, thiamine, riboflavin, vitamin B^6, vitamin B^{12}, vitamin E, folate, calcium, magnesium, copper, and potassium.

Mango Sunrise

Mango Sunrise is high in antioxidants, making it another great choice for the immune system. Wheat germ adds selenium and zinc, which are often lacking in our diets, but you can skip the wheat germ if you'd prefer a smoother textured drink. If you're not an orange juice fan, try substituting cranberry juice or vitamin C-fortified apple juice.

½ mango, cubed
50 ml orange juice
125 ml vanilla-flavoured fortified soya milk
1 tablespoon toasted wheat germ (optional)
dash nutmeg

Combine the mango, orange juice, soya milk, and toasted wheat germ (optional) in a blender and process until smooth. Garnish with freshly ground nutmeg.

yield:

1 serving (250 ml)

per serving without wheat germ:

170 calories, 4 g protein, 36 g carbohydrates, 2 g fat, 0 mg cholesterol, 2 g dietary fibre, 48 mg sodium. High in vitamin A, vitamin B[12], vitamin C, vitamin E, folate. A good source of thiamine, niacin, vitamin B[6], vitamin D, pantothenic acid, calcium, magnesium, and potassium.

per serving with wheat germ:

197 calories, 6 g protein, 39 g carbohydrates, 3 g fat, 0 mg cholesterol, 3 g dietary fibre, 48 mg sodium. High in vitamin A, vitamin B^{12}, vitamin C, vitamin E, folate, thiamine, and magnesium. A good source of riboflavin, niacin, vitamin B^6, vitamin D, pantothenic acid, calcium, iron, potassium, selenium, and zinc.

choosing
a soya milk

Look for a soya milk that's fortified with extra vitamins and minerals. For soya-based drinks or smoothies, I recommend vanilla-flavoured or plain fortified soya milks. Soya Dream is also fortified with beta carotene, vitamin E, and vitamin D; one serving provides 4 per cent of the recommended Daily Value for iron.

soya
on the go

Soya drinks make great alternatives to the usual sugar-laden fizzy drinks we've become accustomed to using when we're on the go. Provamel offer a range of deliciously smooth and refreshing soya fruit drinks called Soya Fruity – available in apple, pear and orange, pineapple and apricot flavours. Packed in handy size prism packs, they are 100 per cent organic and are great drinks for when you're on the move or as a thirst quencher after sport. (See Resources).

Melon Mango Invigorator

Melon Mango Invigorator makes an excellent snack. It's low in calories, a good source of protein, and brimming with vitamin C, vitamin A, and beta carotene. And because it's made with soya milk, it contains isoflavones that can help protect your body against cancer and heart disease. Taste this one before you add sugar — you may find that it's sweet enough just as it is.

½ mango, cubed
80 g cubed cantaloupe melon
125 ml fortified soya milk
1½ teaspoons sugar

Combine ingredients in a blender and purée. Serve.

yield:

1 serving (250 ml)

per serving:

185 calories, 6 g protein, 37 g carbohydrates, 3 g fat, 0 mg cholesterol, 3 g dietary fibre, 62 mg sodium. High in vitamin A, vitamin C, folate, and B^{12}. A good source of protein, carbohydrate, dietary fibre, thiamine, niacin, vitamin B^6, vitamin D, calcium, magnesium, and potassium.

drink to your health

Caribbean Powerhouse

Movie character Rocky Balboa gulped a beverage full of fresh freshly cracked eggs before his runs through the streets of Philadelphia. Today we know that raw eggs can carry hidden bacteria, so this twenty-first century version of Rocky's power drink is made with a sterilized egg product.

125 ml skimmed milk or fortified soya milk
1 banana
50 ml unsweetened pineapple juice
62 g egg substitute
½ teaspoon sugar
¼ teaspoon vanilla extract

Combine ingredients in a blender and purée. Serve.

yield:
1 serving (325 ml)

per serving with skimmed milk:
228 calories, 12 g protein, 45 g carbohydrates, 1 g fat, 2 mg cholesterol, 3 g dietary fibre, 165 mg sodium. High in protein, vitamin B^6, vitamin C, calcium, and potassium. A good source of carbohydrates, dietary fibre, vitamin A, riboflavin, vitamin D, folate, copper, magnesium, and phosphorus.

Hi-Pro

Try this drink instead of using a high-protein powder. The egg substitute, milk, and peanut butter together deliver 19 grams of protein – more than a third of the day's requirement. The peanut butter also adds zinc, folate, and vitamin E. And Hi-Pro is high in calcium, magnesium, and potassium – three minerals that help keep blood pressure under control.

 1 banana
 125 ml skimmed milk
 50 ml pineapple juice
 62 g egg substitute
 2 tablespoons peanut butter
 ½ teaspoon sugar
 ¼ teaspoon vanilla extract

Combine all ingredients in a blender and process until smooth. Serve.

yield:
 1 serving (almost 500 ml)

per serving:
 414 calories, 19 g protein, 52 g carbohydrates, 17 g fat, 3 g sat fat, 2 mg cholesterol, 5 g dietary fibre, 167 mg sodium. High in protein, dietary fibre, riboflavin, niacin, vitamin B^6, vitamin C, folate, calcium, copper, magnesium, and potassium. A good source of vitamin A, thiamine, vitamin D, vitamin E, pantothenic acid, iron, and zinc.

drink to your health

Orange Julia

Add a few simple ingredients to a glass of orange juice and you've made a good thing even better. Nutritional yeast adds selenium and lots of B vitamins; the protein in the powdered milk and egg white makes this drink frothy, creamy, and delicious.

> 250 ml orange juice
> 1 teaspoon powdered nutritional yeast
> 3 to 4 teaspoons powdered skimmed milk
> 4 teaspoons powdered egg white
> dash sugar (optional)

Combine ingredients in a blender and blend for about 30 seconds. Wait a few seconds for the egg white to absorb the liquid, then blend again for a few seconds. Serve.

yield:
> 1 serving (about 375 ml)

per serving:
> 169 calories, 12 g protein, 30 g carbohydrates, 1 g fat, 1 mg cholesterol, 1 g dietary fibre, 141 mg sodium. High in protein, thiamine, riboflavin, niacin, vitamin B^6, vitamin B^{12}, vitamin C, folate, pantothenic acid, and selenium. A good source of vitamin A, magnesium, and potassium.

powdered
egg white

Pasteurized powdered egg white is a safe, convenient alternative to fresh raw egg whites, which may contain salmonella bacteria. Two teaspoons of the product equals one egg white; a 225 g can contains the equivalent of more than 4 dozen whites. It can be stored on the shelf, and you'll never waste yolks again! They even make a nice meringue when mixed with water.

Mike's Blueberry Egg Cream

Egg cream, my son's favourite drink, contains neither egg nor cream. The popular New York beverage is traditionally made from chocolate syrup, milk, and soda water. Here, blueberries replace the chocolate for a drink that's naturally sweet and low in calories. The anti-ageing properties of blueberries can't be beaten, and they help prevent urinary tract infections, too.

> 73 g fresh or 80 g frozen blueberries
> 125 ml skimmed milk or soya milk
> 125 ml soda water

Combine the blueberries and milk in a blender and purée. Pour into a glass and add the soda water. Stir and serve.

yield:
1 serving (250 ml)

per serving with skimmed milk:
92 calories, 5 g protein, 16 g carbohydrates, 2 g fat, 5 mg cholesterol, 2 g dietary fibre, 67 mg sodium. High in B^{12}, vitamin D, and calcium. A good source of riboflavin and vitamin C.

the anti-ageing
power of berries

Blueberries and cranberries contain ellagic acid, a substance that helps to protect us from the free radicals which cause ageing and contribute to or accelerate disease. Berries are also high in vitamin C, the free radical-fighting antioxidant that can help prevent ageing and age-related illnesses such as heart disease, cancer, and even prevent cataracts.

Like blueberries, cranberries are high in ellagic acid, which slows ageing and tumour growth. Cancer and heart disease can be hindered by cranberries, and cranberry juice has a reputation for fighting urinary tract infections. And the flavonoid quercetin helps prevent cancer and free radical damage.

Soya Peach Blueberry Perk-Up

High in fibre, low in fat, and packed with the antioxidant beta carotene, vitamin E, and vitamin C, this drink can help prevent cancer and so much more. Soya protein (from the soya milk) is believed to prevent heart disease, while the combination of protein, magnesium, fibre, and vitamins makes it a good choice for those with chronic fatigue syndrome. The Perk-Up provides two full servings of fruit (remember, five a day) to boot. Cheers!

    125 ml fortified soya milk
    73 g blueberries, fresh or frozen
    1 peach, peeled and quartered or 80 g frozen sliced peach
    1 teaspoon lemon juice
    1 teaspoon nutritional yeast

Combine ingredients in a blender and purée. Serve.

yield:
  1 serving (about 250 ml)

per serving:
  157 calories, 8 g protein, 29 g carbohydrates, 2 g fat, 0 mg cholesterol, 5 g dietary fibre, 58 mg sodium. High in dietary fibre, vitamin A (beta carotene), vitamin E, thiamine, riboflavin, niacin, vitamin B^6, vitamin B^{12}, vitamin C, folate, and pantothenic acid. A good source of protein, carbohydrates, vitamin D, calcium, magnesium, and potassium.

Nutritional yeast, also known as brewer's yeast, is a nutritional supplement that's high in selenium and the B vitamins and can easily be added to your favourite food and beverage recipes. Unlike baker's yeast (the kind used in baking), nutritional yeast does not contain live yeast cultures. It is grown in purified molasses, under strict sanitary conditions and carefully regulated temperatures, then fermented, washed, pasteurized, and dried before it's sold in bags or jars at your local health food shop. I like to use mild-tasting generic yeast flakes for my beverage recipes.

Health Claims For Cancer Prevention On Food Labels

Research confirming the link between diet and cancer convinced America's Food and Drug Administration (FDA) to allow certain foods to carry labels with cancer-fighting claims. According to the 1990 Nutrition Labeling and Education Act, a food product may carry cancer-related health claims on its label if it is

- low in fat, containing 3 or fewer grams of fat per serving or 1 gram or less of saturated fat per serving and less than 95 mg of cholesterol per serving, or
- high in fibre, specifically containing a grain, fruit or vegetable that has 5 grams or more of fibre per serving.

Fruits and vegetables that are low in fat, high in fibre and good sources of vitamins A or C can also be advertised as having cancer-fighting properties.

Mango Milk
with Green Tea

Combine mangoes, which are loaded with vitamins, and green tea, with its powerful antioxidants, and you've got a drink that can help fight cancer and heart disease. Try it as a mid-afternoon snack or as part of a healthy breakfast.

½ mango, cubed
125 ml skimmed milk or soya milk
250 ml green tea
dash nutmeg (garnish)

Combine the ingredients in a blender and process until smooth. Garnish with a dash of nutmeg.

yield:
1 serving (500 ml)

per serving with skimmed milk:
118 calories, 5 g protein, 23 g carbohydrates, 2 g fat, 5 mg cholesterol, 2 g dietary fibre, and 64 mg sodium. High in vitamin A and carotenoids, riboflavin, vitamin B[12], vitamin C, vitamin D, and calcium. A good source of thiamine, vitamin B[6], vitamin E, and folate.

Soya Peach
Strawberry Smoothie

Too tired to fix a full meal? Try this energizing, nutrient-dense smoothie. Low in sodium, high in vitamin A and the B vitamins, and a good source of protein, dietary fibre, and magnesium, this drink is recommended for those with chronic fatigue syndrome. The soya protein base makes it an excellent choice for heart disease prevention, too.

> 125 ml fortified soya milk or skimmed or low-fat milk
> 1 peach, peeled and quartered, or 250 g frozen sliced
>   peaches
> 3 strawberries, fresh or frozen
> 1 tablespoon wheat germ

Combine ingredients in blender and purée. Serve.

yield:
   1 serving (250 ml)

per serving:
   145 calories, 8 g protein, 23 g carbohydrates, 3 g fat, 0 mg cholesterol, 4 g dietary fibre, 53 mg sodium. High in vitamin A, thiamine, vitamin B^{12}, vitamin C, folate, and magnesium. A good source of protein, dietary fibre, riboflavin, niacin, vitamin B^6, vitamin D, pantothenic acid, calcium, iron, potassium, selenium and zinc.

drink to your health

Creamy Orange Pineapple Refresher

Delicious any time, this tropical drink is particularly beneficial when you're suffering from a cold or bacterial infection. It packs a healthy dose of vitamin C, and live cultures in yogurt help replace beneficial bacteria that antibiotics can destroy. Wheat germ adds zinc, another cold fighter. (If you like the orange/pineapple flavour combination but are avoiding dairy, try the Orange Pineapple Refresher recipe on page 125.)

> 125 ml orange juice
> 73 g fresh pineapple chunks or 99 g of canned pineapple
>   chunks (packed in unsweetened juice)
> 125 ml vanilla non-fat yogurt with live cultures
> 1 teaspoon wheat germ

Combine ingredients in a blender and process until smooth. Serve.

yield:
    1 serving (300 ml)

per serving:
    214 calories, 8 g protein, 45 g carbohydrates, 1 g fat, 2 mg cholesterol, 2 g dietary fibre, 86 mg sodium. High in riboflavin, vitamin C, calcium, and a good source of zinc, potassium, protein, carbohydrates, thiamine, vitamin B^6, vitamin B^{12}, folate, pantothenic acid, and magnesium.

Prune-Raisin Smoothie

Prunes and raisins are soaked in hot water, then blended with yogurt and apple sauce to create a fruity beverage that's high in anti-oxidants and an excellent aid for constipation. Fibre, of course, keeps things moving along the digestive tract, while the dihydroxphenylisatin in prunes is a bowel stimulant, and raisins contain tartaric acid, a natural laxative.

> 5 dried prunes, pitted
> 35 g raisins
> 175 ml boiling or hot water
> 50 ml plain non-fat yogurt
> 50 ml unsweetened apple sauce
> dash cinnamon

Soak prunes and raisins in boiling water. After 20 minutes, place in a blender and purée. Add the yogurt, apple sauce, and cinnamon and purée again. Serve.

yield:
  1 serving (375 ml)

per serving:
  286 calories, 6 g protein, 71 g carbohydrates, 1 g fat, 1 mg cholesterol, 5 g dietary fibre, 62 mg sodium. High in vitamin A, riboflavin, calcium, and potassium. A good source of protein, thiamine, niacin, vitamin B^6, vitamin B^{12}, vitamin E, copper, iron, and magnesium.

drink to your health

Blueberry Smoothie

Here's to your heart health: magnesium, calcium, and potassium help keep blood pressure low; flaxseed contributes healthy omega-3 acids to lower unhealthy LDL cholesterol. And with a low-fat dairy base, this smoothie qualifies for the DASH (Dietary Approaches to Stop Hypertension) diet. What's more, the soya protein in the soya milk offers heart protection.

> 240 ml container low-fat or non-fat blueberry yogurt (or
> one 240 ml container vanilla yogurt plus 80 g fresh
> or unsweetened frozen blueberries)
> 125 ml fortified soya milk
> 2 teaspoons ground flaxseed

Combine all ingredients in a blender and process until smooth, or mix well with a spoon or hand whisk. Serve.

yield:
  1 serving (325 ml)

per serving (with blueberry yogurt):
  316 calories, 16 g protein, 52 g carbohydrates, 3 g dietary fibre, 7 g fat, 2 g saturated fat, 10 mg cholesterol, 173 mg sodium. High in riboflavin, vitamin B^{12}, calcium. A good source of vitamin A, thiamine, vitamin E, folate, pantothenic acid, magnesium, potassium, selenium and zinc.

flaxseed

Flaxseed (which comes from flax, the plant used to make linen) can be ground in a coffee grinder and stirred into drinks for added nutritional benefits. Flaxseed is high in fibre and provides healthy omega-3 fatty acids, which can lower levels of 'bad' LDL cholesterol. Also, flax and flaxseed contain lignans, powerful antioxidants that eliminate free radicals and help prevent heart disease, cancer, and menopause symptoms.

Flaxseed is best stored refrigerated or frozen.

Soya Cantaloupe Smoothie

Similar in taste and colour to the popular bottled soya drinks sold in melon, orange, and lime flavours, this smoothie makes a great introduction to soya. In addition to being delicious, it's high in the healing antioxidants (beta carotene, vitamin C, and vitamin E).

125 ml vanilla-flavoured fortified soya milk
50 ml orange juice
80 g cubed cantaloupe, honeydew, or watermelon

Combine the ingredients in a blender and process until smooth.

yield:

1 serving (250 ml)

per serving:

131 calories, 4 g protein, 25 g carbohydrates, 2 g fat, 0 mg cholesterol, 1 g dietary fibre, 53 mg sodium. High in vitamin A, vitamin C, vitamin B^{12}, vitamin E, and folate. A good source of thiamine, vitamin B^6, vitamin D, calcium, magnesium, and potassium.

antioxidants

Antioxidants – vitamins C, E, and A, the mineral selenium, beta carotene and other carotenoids – are compounds found in fruits, vegetables, and whole grains that can actually help fight disease and ageing. How do they do it? Antioxidants protect our bodies from free radicals – the oxygen molecules that are created naturally when our cells produce energy or (less naturally) when our bodies are exposed to harmful toxins in the environment. Left alone, free radicals can damage our healthy cells. Antioxidants bind with free radicals, preventing them from doing further damage.

Antioxidants are measured in units called an ORAC (Oxygen Radical Absorbance Capacity). Research has suggested that in order to reap the benefits of antioxidants, between 3,000 and 5,000 ORAC units should be consumed daily.

drink to your health

fruits high in ORAC units (listed from highest to lowest ORAC content) per 100 g

Prunes	5770
Raisins	2830
Blueberries	2400
Blackberries	2036
Strawberries	1540
Raspberries	1220
Plums	949
Oranges	750
Red grapes	739
Cherries	670
Kiwi	602
Pink grapefruit	483

vegetables high in ORAC units (listed from highest to lowest ORAC content) per 100 g

Kale	1770
Spinach	1260
Brussels sprouts	980
Alfalfa sprouts	930
Broccoli	890
Beetroot	840
Red bell peppers	710
Onion	450
Corn	400
Aubergine	390

Psyllium Soother

Try this fruity, high-fibre drink for constipation relief. Active cultures found in lactose-free milk, acidophilus milk, and yogurt can also help relieve the symptoms of irritable bowel syndrome.

> 160 g cubed cantaloupe melon
> 160 g sliced strawberries
> 125 ml plain non-fat yogurt, lactose-free milk, or
>   acidophilus milk
> 1 teaspoon powdered psyllium

Combine ingredients in blender and purée. Serve immediately.

yield:

1 serving (about 375 ml)

per serving with plain non-fat yogurt:

158 calories, 9 g protein, 32 g carbohydrates, 1 g fat, 2 mg cholesterol, 6 g dietary fibre, 110 mg sodium. High in vitamin A, dietary fibre, riboflavin, vitamin C, folate, calcium, and potassium. A good source of protein, carbohydrates, vitamin B[6], vitamin B[12], folate, magnesium, and zinc.

psyllium

Psyllium, or psyllium seed, is a soluble fibre that may be helpful in lowering blood cholesterol and is recommended for haemorrhoids, irritable bowel syndrome, and constipation. Once ingested, psyllium absorbs water and helps soften stools as they pass through the digestive tract.

Psyllium is the active ingredient in 'natural' over-the-counter laxatives and can be found in some ready-to-eat cereals. You can also buy it in powdered form at health food shops and add it to your favourite beverage.

Some people are allergic to psyllium, so start with a teaspoon and work up to two teaspoons a day if needed. Mix each teaspoon of psyllium with at least 175 ml of any liquid, and drink the mixture quickly before it has a chance to thicken. To ensure proper digestion, drink plenty of fluids when you add psyllium to your diet.

Golden Quencher

Apricots are packed with nutrients, and so is this delicious drink. Beta carotene, which gives apricots their golden-orange colour, helps protect against cancer, heart disease, and stroke. Apricots also contain malic acid, recommended to ease the symptoms associated with fibromyalgia. If you don't have ripe fresh apricots on hand, canned apricots or apricot purée are an equally healthy alternative.

> 3 apricots, pitted and quartered or 125 ml apricot purée
> 125 ml apple juice
> 125 ml fortified soya milk

Combine the ingredients in a blender. Purée. Serve.

yield:
1 serving (375 ml)

per serving:
174 calories, 7 g protein, 33 g carbohydrates, 3 g dietary fibre, 3 g fat, 0 mg cholesterol, 57 mg sodium. High in vitamin A, vitamin B^{12}, and vitamin C. A good source of vitamin E, calcium, iron, magnesium, and potassium.

drink to your health

Avocado Smoothie

This thick, pale green smoothie is nutrient-dense. Avocado and soya protein benefit the heart and blood pressure; orange juice adds vitamin C for healing. And because it's high in magnesium, this drink is recommended for persons with fibromyalgia and chronic fatigue syndrome.

½ ripe avocado
125 ml freshly squeezed orange juice
125 ml fortified soya milk

Remove the skin and the stone from the avocado; place the fruit in a blender. Add the orange juice and soya milk and process until smooth. Pour into a glass and serve.

yield:
1 serving (375 ml)

per serving:
283 calories, 8 g protein, 27 g carbohydrates, 18 g fat, 10 g mono fat, 0 mg cholesterol, 5 g dietary fibre, 64 mg sodium. High in dietary fibre, vitamin A, thiamine, vitamin B^6, vitamin B^{12}, vitamin C, vitamin E, folate, magnesium and potassium. A good source of riboflavin, niacin, pantothenic acid, calcium, copper, and iron.

avocado

Don't be scared off by the relatively high fat content in avocado-based drinks. Avocado is a healthy source of 'good' monounsaturated fat, which can actually lower blood cholesterol. And half an avocado has more blood-pressure regulating potassium than a medium-size banana. If fat is an issue for you, look for Florida avocados, which contain about half the fat found in their California cousins. (Talk to your supermarket produce manager or look for stickers indicating where grown.)

A ripe avocado is slightly soft – it should yield somewhat under gentle finger pressure. (Harder avocados will ripen in a few days at room temperature.) Store a ripe avocado in the refrigerator and use it as soon as possible. Once cut, an avocado will turn brown unless it is treated with lemon juice or tightly wrapped and refrigerated.

drink to your health

Ginger Mango Supersmoothie

This is one powerful drink! Superhealer antioxidants (vitamins A, C, and E, beta carotene, and selenium) and live yogurt cultures give your immune system a terrific boost. Ginger adds kick and can help relieve migraine headaches, stomach distress, and motion sickness. And calcium, magnesium, and potassium help keep blood pressure low.

> 1 mango
> 125 ml plain non-fat yogurt
> 125 ml hot ginger tea, cooled (see page 203)
> ⅛ teaspoon ground nutmeg

Peel and core the mango and drop into a blender. Add the yogurt and ginger tea. Blend. Pour into a glass, adding ice if desired. Top with ground nutmeg.

yield:
> 1 serving (250 ml)

per serving:
> 205 calories, 8 g protein, 45 g carbohydrates, 1 g fat, 2 mg cholesterol, 4 g dietary fibre, 101 mg sodium. High in vitamin A, riboflavin, vitamin C, and calcium. A good source of protein, carbohydrates, fibre, thiamine, vitamin B⁶, vitamin B¹², vitamin E, folate, pantothenic acid, copper, magnesium, potassium and selenium.

Island Powerhouse

Tropical fruits are nutritional powerhouses – they're loaded with fibre, phytochemicals, and vitamins. This pineapple and papaya smoothie brings you a taste of the islands and a healthy dose of vitamin C. (To make your own fresh papaya purée, add peeled cubed papaya to the blender with 2–3 tablespoons of water and purée.)

> 75 ml papaya purée, fresh or bottled
> 75 ml pineapple juice
> 75 ml non-fat vanilla yogurt

Combine the ingredients in a bowl and mix well with a wire whisk. Serve.

yield:
> 1 serving (250 ml)

per serving:
> 149 calories, 5 g protein, 33 g carbohydrates, 0.3 g fat, 1 mg cholesterol, 2 g dietary fibre, 59 mg sodium. High in vitamin A and vitamin C. A good source of riboflavin, folate, calcium, protein, carbohydrates and potassium.

Morning Superstart

If you can't take time out for a full breakfast, this satisfying, nutrient-dense drink is for you. It contains all the ingredients of a typical breakfast: fruit, juice, cereal, coffee, and dairy. Drink it on the run if you have to — you'll be glad you got off to a healthy start!

> 240 ml container low-fat or non-fat coffee yogurt
> (or 240 ml plain low-fat or non-fat yogurt plus
> 1 teaspoon powdered instant coffee)
> 50 ml apricot purée
> 2 fresh apricots, pitted, or 2 canned pitted apricots
> 2 tablespoons toasted wheat germ
> 1 teaspoon cocoa powder
> 1/8 teaspoon cinnamon

Combine ingredients in a blender and process until smooth. Serve.

yield:

1 serving (500 ml)

per serving with low-fat yogurt:

321 calories, 17 g protein, 54 g carbohydrates, 5 g fat, 2 g saturated fat, 11 mg cholesterol, 4 g dietary fibre, 153 mg sodium. High in protein, vitamin A, thiamine, riboflavin, vitamin B^{12}, folate, calcium, magnesium, potassium, selenium, and zinc. A good source of carbohydrates, dietary fibre, vitamin B^6, vitamin C, vitamin E, pantothenic acid, copper, and iron.

Chocolate Kiwi Surprise

Chocolate and kiwi? Try it and see! This rich-tasting smoothie is a delicious source of vitamin C, dietary fibre, and potassium. Like soya milk, rice milk should be stored at room temperature until opening. Or make your own rice milk (see Rice Cure, p.181). Because it's high in fibre and wheat- and dairy-free, this drink is a good choice for persons with irritable bowel syndrome.

> 250 ml chocolate-flavoured rice milk (or 250 ml plain rice
>   milk plus 2–3 teaspoons of chocolate syrup)
> 1 kiwi, peeled
> 1 banana, cut into chunks

Combine ingredients in a blender and process until smooth. Serve.

yield:
1 serving (about 500 ml)

per serving:
325 calories, 3 g protein, 75 g carbohydrates, 4 g fat, 0 mg cholesterol, 7 g dietary fibre, 120 mg sodium. High in vitamin C, dietary fibre, carbohydrates, and potassium. A good source of vitamin E, folate, copper, and magnesium.

Kiwi Soya Smoothie

So simple, yet so good for you! This smoothie is loaded with nutrients. It's a fine source of dietary fibre, too.

1 kiwi
250 ml fortified soya milk

Peel the kiwi, cut it into quarters and combine with the soya milk in a blender. Blend and serve.

yield:

1 serving (250 ml)

per serving:

176 calories, 11 g protein, 24 g carbohydrate, 4 g fat, 0 mg cholesterol, 3 g dietary fibre, 109 mg sodium. High in protein, vitamin A, vitamin C, vitamin B^{12}, vitamin E, calcium, magnesium, and potassium. A good source of dietary fibre, thiamine, vitamin B^6, vitamin D, folate, and iron.

Kiwi Strawberry Smoothie

Add strawberries to the Kiwi Soya Smoothie and you'll get more than just delightful flavour. Strawberries add pantothenic acid, copper, and phytochemicals that strengthen the immune system. Try this one for relief of PMS symptoms – it's high in vitamin E, calcium, and magnesium. The vitamin B^6 and carbohydrates can also help relieve stress and regulate mood swings. With fructose for quick energy, it can even aid in hangover recovery.

1 ripe kiwi, peeled
148 g sliced strawberries
250 ml fortified soya milk
1 packet or ¾ teaspoon fructose

Add ingredients to blender, purée, and serve.

yield:
1 serving (500 ml)

per serving:
231 calories, 12 g protein, 37 g carbohydrates, 5 g fat, 0 mg cholesterol, 6 g dietary fibre, 111 mg sodium. High in dietary fibre, vitamin A, vitamin B^{12}, vitamin C, vitamin E, folate, calcium, magnesium, and potassium. A good source of carbohydrates, thiamine, riboflavin, vitamin B^6, vitamin D, pantothenic acid, copper, and iron.

drink to your health

Mighty Blue Healer

The healing powers of this tasty blue drink are mighty indeed. It's brimming with healing phytochemicals and healthy B vitamins.

125 ml soya milk
73 g fresh blueberries
125 ml orange juice
1 teaspoon ground flaxseed, psyllium, or bran

Purée in blender and serve cold.

yield:
1 serving (250 ml)

per serving:
146 calories, 7 g protein, 25 g carbohydrates, 4 g fat, 0 mg cholesterol, 4 g dietary fibre, 58 mg sodium. High in vitamin B^{12} and vitamin C. A good source of protein, dietary fibre, vitamin A, thiamine, vitamin E, folate, calcium, magnesium and potassium.

High potassium, that is. One serving of this fruity pink drink supplies 900 mg of potassium, almost half the day's 2000 milligram requirement. Potassium helps prevent high blood pressure, promotes muscle contraction, and is important in maintaining the fluid and electrolyte balance in our cells. Try it for a midday pick-me-up.

 1 ripe banana
 6 strawberries
 250 ml apple juice
 4 teaspoons lemon or lime juice

Add ingredients to blender and blend. Serve.

yield:
 1 serving (375 ml)

per serving:
 252 calories, 2 g protein, 64 g carbohydrates, 2 g fat, 0 mg cholesterol, 5 g dietary fibre, 10 mg sodium. High in carbohydrates, dietary fibre, vitamin B^6, and vitamin C, folate, and potassium. A good source of thiamine, riboflavin, iron, and magnesium.

Pear and Blueberry Smoothie

This fruity, refreshing smoothie tastes so good you'll forget you are drinking something nutritious! And nutritious it is, with the healing power of blueberries, soya, and yogurt with live cultures. Sunflower seeds are a wonderful source of the antioxidant selenium and heart-healthy magnesium.

½ pear, peeled
73 g blueberries
125 ml fortified soya milk
125 ml plain skimmed yogurt
1 tablespoon unsalted sunflower seeds

Combine the ingredients in a blender and purée. Serve.

yield:
1 serving (375 ml)

per serving:
270 calories, 14 g protein, 41 g carbohydrates, 7 g fat, 2 mg cholesterol, 5 g dietary fibre, 151 mg sodium. High in protein, riboflavin, vitamin B[12], vitamin C, vitamin E, calcium, and potassium. A good source of dietary fibre, carbohydrates, vitamin A, thiamine, vitamin B[6], folate, pantothenic acid, copper, magnesium, selenium, and zinc.

Soya Do It

Try this refreshing, light-green drink along with a few slices of whole-wheat toast for a healthy, well-rounded breakfast. With 40 milligrams of isoflavones, Soya Do It can help relieve menopausal symptoms and protect against heart disease. Calcium, potassium, and magnesium are good for your blood pressure, and tropical fruits provide fibre and immune-boosting vitamin C.

>   1 kiwi, peeled
>   250 ml fortified soya milk
>   73 g fresh cubed pineapple
>   125 ml orange juice
>   pineapple slice (for garnish)

Add ingredients to blender and purée. Garnish with pineapple slice.

yield:
1 serving (375 ml)

per serving:
270 calories, 12 g protein, 47 g carbohydrates, 5 g fat, 0 mg cholesterol, 4 g dietary fibre, 111 mg sodium. High in protein, vitamin A, vitamin C, vitamin E, folate, calcium, magnesium, and potassium. A good source of carbohydrates, dietary fibre, vitamin D, copper, iron, and isoflavones.

Purple Protein Power Shake

A high-protein drink can help you keep your mind on your work — try one or two servings of this purple shake for lunch, and see how you feel that afternoon. It may help elevate your mood, too: vitamin B^{12} and folate help your body convert the methionine found in soya into mood-enhancing SAMe.

> 250 ml vanilla flavoured fortified soya milk
> 175 g firm tofu
> 146 g fresh or 161 g frozen, unthawed blueberries
> 50 ml orange juice
> 6 tablespoons soya protein powder (optional)

Combine all ingredients in a blender and process until smooth. Serve.

yield:
> 2 servings (375 ml each)

per serving without protein powder:
> 221 calories, 13 g protein, 31 g carbohydrates, 5 g fat, 0 mg cholesterol, 2 g dietary fibre, 95 mg sodium. High in protein, vitamin B^{12}, vitamin C, and a good source of vitamin A, thiamine, folate, calcium, copper, iron, magnesium, and potassium.

per serving with protein powder:
> 268 calories, 21 g protein, 36 g carbohydrates, 5 g fat, 0 mg cholesterol, 3 g dietary fibre, 96 mg sodium. High in protein, thiamine, vitamin B^{12}, vitamin C, folate, calcium, copper, iron, magnesium, phosphorus, potassium, and a good source of dietary fibre, vitamin A and zinc.

Cocoa Fruit Smoothie

This nutrient-dense drink will fill you up and lift your spirits! Cocoa produces mood-enhancing endorphins, and vitamins B^6, B^{12}, and folate help your body produce SAMe from the methionine found in soya. With soya protein and lots of carbohydrates, this drink may help relieve PMS symptoms, as well.

> ½ banana, cut into chunks
> 1 peach, peeled and sliced, or 250 g sliced peaches
> (251 g unsweetened frozen peaches or 218 g
> canned and packed in juice)
> 2 teaspoons rich cocoa powder
> 250 ml vanilla-flavoured fortified soya milk

Combine all ingredients in a blender and purée until smooth.

yield:
1 serving (375 ml)

per serving:
260 calories, 8 g protein, 50 g carbohydrates, 4 g fat, 0 mg cholesterol, 4 g dietary fibre, 92 mg sodium. High in vitamin A, dietary fibre, vitamin B^6, vitamin B^{12}, vitamin C, vitamin D, vitamin E, folate, calcium, magnesium, and potassium. A good source of protein, carbohydrates, thiamine, riboflavin, niacin, pantothenic acid, copper, and iron.

Mellow Mama

Turn to dairy-free, soya-free Mellow Mama for relief from the stresses and symptoms of Premenstrual Syndrome. Fruits, vegetables, and nuts provide calming carbohydrates; the antioxidant vitamins A, C, and E are also recommended for PMS. Make your own almond milk (see page 176) or buy it at your local health food shop.

> 27 g raw spinach, washed and drained
> 1 orange, peeled and sectioned
> 50 ml almond milk
> 1 teaspoon honey
> ½ teaspoon lemon juice
> ¼ teaspoon mustard

Combine all ingredients in a blender and purée until smooth.

yield:
  1 serving

per serving:
  123 calories, 3 g protein, 23 g carbohydrates, 3 g fat, 0 mg cholesterol, 4 g dietary fibre, 29 mg sodium. High in vitamin A, vitamin C, and a good source of fibre, vitamin E, folate, magnesium, and potassium.

3

Tea, whether green, black, or herbal, contains disease-fighting compounds and can often provide relief for specific ailments. Use loose tea leaves or convenient bags; blend different kinds of teas or add spices and juices to create new flavours. Soothing and hot or refreshing and iced, the teas in this chapter are healthy and easy to prepare.

teas, infusions, tisanes, and coffees

Lemon Balm
Anxiety Reducer

A hot cup of tea, slowly prepared, held, and consumed, can do wonders to soothe the mind, body, and spirit. Lemon balm is particularly calming and can help with anxiety and insomnia.

> 2 teaspoons or 1 bag lemon balm tea
> 2 teaspoons or 1 bag chamomile tea
> 1 teaspoon or 1 bag peppermint tea
> 500 ml boiling water
> ginger syrup (see page 202) or mint syrup (see page 204)
>   to taste

Combine the teas in a cup or teapot. Pour boiling water over the tea and steep for 4 to 5 minutes. Strain. Add ginger or mint syrup to taste. Serve.

yield:
2 servings (250 ml each)

per serving:
2 calories, 0 g protein, 1 g carbohydrates, 0 g fat, 0 mg cholesterol, 0 g dietary fibre, 2 mg sodium.

infusions

An infusion is a term for a tea prepared by pouring boiling water over fresh or dried herbs. The hot water is infused with the essence of the herbs by steeping. An infusion and a tisane are the same.

Doubly Green Tea

Cool and refreshing, this lime-green iced tea delivers a hefty dose of antioxidant polyphenols and 23 per cent of the recommended Daily Value of vitamin C. This tea is also good for the heart and circulatory system; vitamin C may help lower cholesterol, while the bioflavonoids in lime and other citrus juices may protect the blood vessels and act as blood thinners.

> 250 ml boiling water
> 1–2 teaspoons loose green tea or 1 bag green tea
> 3 tablespoons lime juice
> 4 packets (3 teaspoons) fructose or 3 teaspoons sugar or
>   sugar substitute to taste
> ice

Pour the boiled water over the loose tea or tea bag; steep for 2 to 3 minutes. Strain and allow to cool. Pour the lime juice into a tall glass. Add the fructose, sugar, or sugar substitute and stir to dissolve. Add the green tea and stir again. Add ice to fill the glass. Serve.

yield:
   1 serving (250 ml)

per serving:
   57 calories, 0.2 g protein, 16 g carbohydrates, 0.1 g fat, 0 mg cholesterol, 0.2 g dietary fibre, 9 mg sodium. High in vitamin C.

green tea

Green tea is believed to prevent cancer and heart disease, lower cholesterol, and even prevent tooth decay. To brew a perfect cup of green tea, bring 250 ml of water to a boil, then allow it to cool slightly before pouring it over 1 to 2 teaspoons of tea leaves or a tea bag. (Loose green tea generally produces a stronger brew than a tea bag will.) Let the tea steep for just one or two minutes before straining it.

If you make green tea often, consider buying a small, Japanese-style teapot with a built-in strainer – it's a marvellous time-saver. In Japan, green tea leaves are re-used for second cups or pots of tea; they're just steeped a bit longer the second time around.

the power of polyphenols

Both green and black teas contain powerful polyphenols, anti-oxidants thought to prevent cancer and heart disease. But the polyphenols in green tea are more plentiful and easier for our bodies to absorb, earning green tea its star polyphenol status.

You can get your polyphenols by drinking hot, iced, or caffeine-free green tea. Bottled green tea-based beverages contain fewer polyphenols, but they do deliver some.

Echinacea Tea with Lemon and Honey

Next time you have a cold, try this soothing, immune-boosting tea. In fact, drink a cup at least three times a day until you're feeling better. Hot tea and honey will heat you up, make you sweat, and relieve throat pain and discomfort. Echinacea is particularly noted for its ability to fight infections and may lessen the intensity and duration of a cold. It also helps clear mucous from the throat. Echinacea does dry out your mouth and nasal passages, so drink more water and juices when taking it.

To make a basic echinacea tea, pour 250 ml of boiling water over 2 teaspoons of dried echinacea and steep for 3 to 5 minutes. Add other herbs and spices for improved flavour.

> 500 ml boiling water
> 1 tablespoon loose echinacea or 1 bag echinacea tea
> 1 teaspoon peppermint tea or 1 bag peppermint tea
> 1 teaspoon dried chamomile flowers or 1 bag chamomile tea
> 1 teaspoon honey
> 2 teaspoons fresh lemon juice

Pour boiling water over the loose tea or tea bags and steep for 3 to 5 minutes. Remove bags or strain, then add the honey and lemon. Sip this tea while it's hot – the heat is helpful in healing as well.

yield:

2 servings (250 ml each)

per serving:

23 calories, 0 g protein, 6 g carbohydrates, 0 g fat, 0 mg cholesterol, 0 g dietary fibre, 7 mg sodium.

Licorice Root Soother

Licorice root contains glycyrrhizic acid, a decongestant that helps reduce inflammation and loosen mucous, making this an excellent tea for colds, coughs, or bronchitis. Experts also believe that licorice root may be responsible for the production of interferon, which helps our bodies fight off infections.

Despite its name, licorice root is flavourless on its own; the fennel seed in this recipe produces that traditional 'licorice' flavour. Fennel is a soothing spice, as are cardamom and cinnamon.

Caution: Licorice root can raise blood pressure and should not be taken by those on blood pressure medication. Excessive amounts of licorice root – more than 50 g a day – can be harmful for those persons with liver disease or chronic hepatitis, those taking diuretics or steroids, and pregnant women.

> 1 bag licorice root tea or 1 dried licorice root stick
> 3–4 dried mint leaves or 1–2 teaspoons dried mint or 1
>   bag mint tea
> ¼ teaspoon crushed fennel seed
> pinch cardamom
> pinch cinnamon
> 250 ml water
> 1 teaspoon honey

If you're using a licorice root tea bag: place the tea bag in a mug, along with the mint, fennel, cardamom, cinnamon. Add boiling water, and let steep for 3 to 5 minutes. Strain. Add honey, mix well, and serve.

If you're using dried licorice root stick: break one 4-inch dried

drink to your health

licorice root stick into inch-long pieces. Place the pieces in 500 ml of water and bring to a boil; lower the heat and simmer for 15 minutes. Strain tea and pour 250 ml into a cup or teapot. Add mint, fennel, cardamom, and cinnamon, then steep for 3 to 5 minutes. Add honey, mix well, and serve.

yield:

1 serving (250 ml)

per serving:

2 calories, 0 g protein, 0.3 g carbohydrates, 0 g fat, 0 mg cholesterol, 0 g dietary fibre, 2 mg sodium.

decoctions

Herbal decoctions are made by boiling herbs in water to extract their flavours and essences. The decoction method is used when making tea from dried twigs or roots.

Greenberry Tea

Fruit-leaf teas are easy to prepare and can help alleviate digestive problems. To make a basic fruit-leaf tea, steep blackberry, blueberry, or raspberry leaves in boiling water for 5 minutes, strain, and serve. In this recipe, berry leaves are teamed with antioxidant-rich green tea to boost your immune system and soothe your stomach. (This tea can help stop diarrhoea, too.)

> 250 ml boiling water
> 1 teaspoon green tea leaves or 1 bag green tea
> 1–2 teaspoons dried blackberry, blueberry, or raspberry
>   leaves
> 1–2 teaspoons fruit syrup (optional)

Pour boiling water over the leaves or tea bag and steep for 3 to 5 minutes. Strain. Serve. One or two teaspoons of fruit syrup can be added for sweetening and flavour if desired.

yield:
> 1 serving (250 ml)

per serving:
> 2 calories, 0 g protein, 0.5 g carbohydrates, 0 g fat, 0 mg cholesterol, 0 g dietary fibre, 2 mg sodium.

echinacea

The herb echinacea (eh-kin-AY-shee-a), which comes from the purple coneflower, is believed to fight infection and boost the immune system. The species *echinacea purpurea* has also been shown to help fight urinary tract infections and to re-establish white blood cell count after cancer treatment.

Do not take or drink echinacea in any form if you are allergic to coneflowers, or if you have multiple sclerosis, AIDS, tuberculosis, leukaemia or autoimmune diseases like rheumatoid arthritis and lupus.

drink to your health

Watermelon Chamomile Frosty

This summer refresher delivers the healing powers of chamomile and the vitamin C of watermelon. And it tastes great, too! To make frozen watermelon cubes, freeze puréed watermelon in ice cube trays. The ice cubes can be stored in sealed plastic bags in the freezer. Keep a cold pitcher of chamomile tea in the refrigerator and making this drink is a snap.

Caution: Chamomile allergies can develop if you are allergic to ragweed.

> 125 ml chamomile tea, cooled
> 231 g frozen watermelon cubes
> 1 teaspoon psyllium powder
> 2 teaspoons mint syrup (optional, see page 204)

Start with cooled tea so it won't melt the frozen watermelon cubes. Pour cool tea into a blender with the frozen watermelon cubes. Purée and add psyllium, blend again, and serve immediately. Add mint syrup if desired.

This recipe can be doubled or tripled successfully.

yield:
1 serving (375 ml)

per serving:
59 calories, 1 g protein, 15 g carbohydrates, 1 g fat, 0 mg cholesterol, 3 g dietary fibre, 6 mg sodium. High in vitamin C. A good source of dietary fibre, vitamin A, and vitamin B[6].

teas, infusions, tisanes and coffees

chamomile

Calming chamomile can help bronchitis, colds, coughs, fever, sore throat, and inflammation. It is also used to promote a good night's sleep. Hot chamomile tea also alleviates cramping and eases the associated discomfort of diarrhoea.

To make basic chamomile tea, place 1 to 2 teaspoons of dried chamomile or one chamomile tea bag in a pot or mug. Add 250 ml of boiling water and steep for 3 to 5 minutes. Strain and serve.

Basil Tea

Drink a cup of this basil tea before a meal to reduce gas or have one after a meal to aid digestion. Basil contains eugenol, a compound that may help reduce muscle spasms and ease cramps and other forms of stomach distress.

This is a strong tea, so don't let it steep too long. I like its clean flavour, but you might try adding peppermint or spearmint for a gentler taste. Or add stomach-friendly lactose-free milk to sweeten it. If wind is a problem, steer clear of sugar or honey.

> 1–2 teaspoons dried basil or 3–4 leaves fresh basil
> 250 ml boiling water
> lactose-free milk (optional)

Pour boiling water over the basil and steep for 8–10 minutes. Strain and serve.

yield:
> 1 serving (250 ml)

per serving:
> 2 calories, 0 g protein, 0 g carbohydrates, 0 g fat, 0 mg cholesterol, 0 g dietary fibre, 0 mg sodium.

tisanes

A tisane (ti-ZAN) is a French name for a tea made from an infusion of fresh or dried herbs. Alice Waters, owner of Chez Panisse restaurant and café in Berkeley, California, is renowned for the tisanes she serves. She pours very hot water over fresh herbs and allows them to steep for 4 or 5 minutes. Fresh herbal tisanes are beautiful prepared in a glass pot and served in glass teacups.

Spirit-Lifting
St John's Wort Tea

Acting much like the commercial drug Prozac and related anti-depressants, St John's Wort is believed to enhance the serotonin level in the brain and relieve feelings of depression. Fortified soya milk in this recipe adds not only flavour but also carbohydrates, vitamin B^6 and vitamin B^{12} – all depression fighters – plus the antioxidant vitamin E.

Try a cup of this tea daily and see how you feel. If you don't detect improvement within a month, stop drinking it.

Caution: Do not take St John's Wort if you are pregnant, taking Nardil or other MAO inhibitors, the HIV medicine Indavir, or the transplant drug Cyclosporin, or birth control medication, as there can be a loss of therapeutic effect.

> 2 teaspoons St John's Wort or 1 bag St John's Wort tea
> 250 ml boiling water
> 50 ml plain fortified soya milk
> ½ teaspoon honey

Pour boiling water over the herb or tea bag and steep for 2 to 3 minutes. Strain or remove the bag; add the soya milk and honey. Serve.

yield:
1 serving (300 ml)

per serving:
45 calories, 3 g protein, 7 g carbohydrates, 1 g fat, 0 mg cholesterol, 0 g dietary fibre, 28 mg sodium. High in vitamin B^{12}. A good source of vitamin E.

Iced Mochaccino

You'll probably agree that there are times when coffee and caffeine are appropriate. In the middle of the day, when energy ebbs, there is nothing like a cup of coffee. I love the smell of coffee in the morning, and reading the morning paper while holding and sipping from a warm mug is one of life's little pleasures.

Coffee can help relieve the tiredness and headache associated with a hangover. Iced Mochaccino contains several hangover helpers: caffeine (in the strong coffee and chocolate), fructose (in the chocolate syrup and whipped topping) and ice, which can provide headache relief by helping dilated blood vessels contract.

> 250 ml strong coffee
> 2 tablespoons chocolate syrup
> 2 teaspoons powdered egg white (see page 50)
> 2 tablespoons warm water
> 2 packages fructose or 1½ teaspoons powdered fructose
> ice
> milk or cream as needed or preferred

Prepare strong coffee by using twice the amount of coffee grounds you usually use when brewing coffee – use 2 tablespoons of coffee for every 250 ml of water. Combine 250 ml of brewed coffee and the chocolate syrup in a tall glass. Stir, and add ice to fill the glass.

In a bowl, combine warm water and the powdered egg white (do not use fresh, uncooked egg white, which can carry salmonella). Stir slowly for 2 minutes, allowing the egg white to absorb the water. Use a wire whisk to beat until foamy; add the fructose and continue whisking until

drink to your health

it is absorbed. Pour this froth into the glass of iced mochaccino and serve.

yield:

1 serving (250 ml)

per serving:

146 calories, 5 g protein, 31 g carbohydrates, 0.4 g fat, 0 mg cholesterol, 1 g dietary fibre, 81 mg sodium, 146 mg caffeine. A good source of protein and carbohydrates.

fructose

Try using powdered or crystalline fructose to sweeten beverages when you want a quick burst of energy. Your body can absorb fructose, the sugar found naturally in fruit and in honey, more quickly than it can absorb sucrose, or table sugar. Fructose is one and a half times as sweet as table sugar, so you won't need to use as much.

Green Ginger Tea

Add zing to a cup of healing green tea with spicy fresh ginger. Because it contains caffeine, this tea is also a good choice if you have a headache. Use a special ginger grater, sold in Asian supermarkets, to grate your ginger. Or chop or slice the ginger then mince it in a garlic press.

> 1 teaspoon grated or minced fresh ginger or ¼ teaspoon
>   powdered ginger
> 1–2 teaspoons loose green tea or 1 bag green tea
> 250 ml boiling water, cooled slightly
> sugar or honey to taste

Add the fresh or dried ginger and the green tea to a mug. Pour slightly cooled water over the tea and steep for 2 to 4 minutes. Strain if you're using the loose tea, and add sugar or honey to taste. Serve immediately or chill and serve over ice.

yield:

1 serving (250 ml)

per serving:

2 calories, 0 g protein, 0.3 g carbohydrates, 0 g fat, 0 mg cholesterol, 0 g dietary fibre, 7 mg sodium

Aromatic Astragalus Tea

Astragalus root, a popular herb in Chinese medicine, is an immune system booster that's believed to increase the production of T-cells, which are among the body's first lines of defence against disease. Astragalus root is useful in combating colds and flu and in treating fatigue, arthritis and diarrhoea. You can buy astragalus in convenient tea bag form, or prepare your own tea by placing one tablespoon of astragalus root (found in Chinese markets) in 250 ml of water and boiling for 15 to 20 minutes.

The herb has an unusual odour – it smells somewhat like cooked corn silk. In this recipe it is combined with jasmine tea, which adds a pleasant aromatic quality and antioxidant flavonoids. The echinacea in this tea helps fight colds or infection as well.

    1 bag astragalus tea
    1–2 teaspoons jasmine tea or 1 bag jasmine tea
    1–2 teaspoons dried loose echinacea
    250 ml boiling water

Pour the boiling water over the teas and steep for 2 to 3 minutes. Remove the bags and strain the tea. Serve with honey if desired.

yield:

    1 serving (250 ml)

per serving:

    2 calories, 0 g protein, 0 g carbohydrates, 0 g fat, 0 mg cholesterol, 0 g dietary fibre, 0 mg sodium.

drink to your health

Green Tea with Punch

This healthful punch combines two heavy-hitting immune system boosters, green tea and vitamin C (you'll get 40 milligrams in each serving). It promotes heart health, as well: green tea can help lower blood pressure and reduce the risk of stroke.

> 500 ml boiling water, slightly cooled
> 2 teaspoons loose green tea or 2 bags of green tea
> 500 ml cranberry juice
> 550 ml pineapple juice
> ice

Prepare the tea by pouring the slightly cooled water over the tea or tea bags in a pot or bowl. Steep for 4 minutes, then strain and cool. Add the cranberry juice and pineapple juice to the cooled tea. Serve over ice.

yield:
> 6 servings (250 ml)

per serving:
> 101 calories, 0.3 g protein, 25 g carbohydrates, 0 mg cholesterol, 0.3 g dietary fibre, 5 mg sodium. High in vitamin C.

Passion Flower Bedtime Tea

Try a cup of this calming, aromatic tea about thirty minutes before bedtime. Passion flower, which grows naturally on vines in the southeastern United States and south to Brazil and Argentina, is known for its soothing properties. This tea will reduce anxiety and ensure a good night's sleep.

> 250 ml boiling water
> 1 bag passion flower tea
> 1 teaspoon dried lemon balm
> 1 teaspoon honey

Pour the boiling water over the tea and steep for 3 to 5 minutes (for a stronger taste, steep up to 10 minutes). Strain or remove the tea bag, add honey, and serve.

yield:
  1 serving (250 ml)

per serving:
  23 calories, 0 g protein, 6 g carbohydrates, 0 g fat, 0 mg cholesterol, 0 g dietary fibre, 3 mg sodium.

drink to your health

Grandmother Rose's Cup of Tea

My grandmother had two favourite cures for insomnia: the bottle of blackberry brandy she kept in her closet and this drink, which she called her 'cup of tea'. She drank this every night, after she set the table for breakfast. I always wondered why she called it tea — there isn't a drop of tea in it. Regardless, it seemed to do the trick and achieved the desired effect.

>   250 ml boiling water
>   2–3 tablespoons low-fat or skimmed milk

Combine in a mug and sip slowly.

yield:
>   1 serving (250 ml)

per serving with low-fat skimmed milk:
>   13 calories, 1 g protein, 2 g carbohydrates, 0.3 g fat, 1 mg cholesterol, 0 g dietary fibre, 23 mg sodium.

Soothing
Spearmint Tea

A patch of spearmint grows in my summer garden, and I'm always surprised at the number of people who recognize it and pull off a leaf to chew. Enjoy this chamomile and spearmint tea after dinner. Spearmint leaves have long been considered a folk remedy for wind. The fennel seeds help humour the stomach and are particularly recommended for those with irritable bowel syndrome.

Caution: People with allergies to ragweed and its relatives should avoid chamomile.

> ½ teaspoon fennel seeds, toasted or untoasted
> 2 teaspoons chamomile or 1 bag chamomile tea
> 2–3 teaspoons of spearmint tea leaves or 1 bag spearmint
>   tea
> 250 ml boiling water
> 1 teaspoon mint syrup, if desired

Crush the fennel seeds and combine with chamomile and spearmint tea leaves or bags in a cup. Add boiling water and steep for 3 to 4 minutes. Strain and serve.

yield:
  1 serving (250 ml)

per serving (estimated):
  15 calories, 1 g protein, 2 g carbohydrates, 0 g fat, 0 mg cholesterol, 0 g dietary fibre, 12 mg sodium.

drink to your health

fennel seeds

Fennel seeds, which have an anise or licorice-like flavour, are believed to hasten digestion and are among the seeds traditionally chewed after meals in India. Buy fennel seeds in the spices section of your supermarket. For better flavour, try toasting them: place seeds in a dry skillet and heat for a minute or two, stirring to prevent burning. Cool the seeds and store them in a sealed container.

To make a basic fennel tea, pour 250 ml of boiling water (or hot milk) over toasted fennel seeds. Steep for 10 minutes. Strain the tea and drink it before meals.

moroccan spearmint tea

Esther Press McManus, now a chef and cooking teacher in Philadelphia, tells me that sugar-sweetened spearmint tea is a popular cure-all in her native Morocco. In her favourite recipe, McManus combines spearmint tea with green tea and adds dried verbena from her garden.

Grape Tea

You could be traditional and add water to your frozen grape juice concentrate. But for added phytochemicals *and* great taste, why not use green tea instead? Tangy Grape Tea is refreshing and packed with immune-system strengtheners.

> 1.075 litres brewed green tea (three 360 ml frozen-juice
>   cans full of tea)
> 360 ml frozen grape juice

Prepare the juice by mixing grape concentrate with three cans (1.075 l) of green tea. Mix well and serve cold.

yield:

12 servings (125 ml each)

per serving:

52 calories, 0.2 g protein, 13 g carbohydrates, 0 g fat, 0 mg cholesterol, 0 g dietary fibre, 5 mg sodium. High in vitamin C.

drink to your health

Heart Soothing Chai

Spicy chai (pronounced *ch-eye*), a beverage originating from the Himalayan mountain regions of Asia, is a rich-tasting mixture of tea, spices, milk, and sugar. Commercial chai can be heavily sweetened and is usually made with black tea. Instead, try this heart-healthy version, made with green tea and soya milk. Serve it hot, or cold over ice.

125 ml water
3 crushed allspice seeds
3 cloves, crushed
pinch cinnamon
pinch powdered ginger
1 bag or 1–2 teaspoons loose green tea
125 ml fortified vanilla-flavoured soya milk
½–1 teaspoon brown sugar or honey

Pour the water in a cup and add the allspice, cloves, cinnamon, and ginger. Microwave for 1 minute on high power. Remove from the microwave and add the tea bag or green tea; steep for 2 to 3 minutes, then strain. Add the soya milk and brown sugar. Serve.

To make this tea without a microwave, mix the spices with the water and bring to a boil on the cooker. Place 1 to 2 teaspoons of green tea or a tea bag in a small pot or cup; pour the spiced water over the tea and steep for several minutes. Strain, add the soya milk and brown sugar, and serve.

Chai can be served warm or over ice.

yield:
1 serving (250 ml)

per serving with vanilla-flavoured soya milk:

85 calories, 3 g protein, 14 g carbohydrates, 2 g fat, 0 mg cholesterol, 0 g dietary fibre, 50 mg sodium. High in vitamin B^{12} and vitamin E. A good source of vitamin A, vitamin D, folate, and calcium.

Lemongrass Ginger Tea

The inspiration for this mild, relaxing tea comes from the *True Thai* cookbook, written by Theresa Volpe Laursen, her husband Byron, and Victor Sodsook, a Thai chef and the owner of the Siamese Princess restaurant in Los Angeles. You can find fresh lemongrass at Asian food shops, but use the dried variety if you must. Crystallized ginger imparts a nice flavour. This tea is also delicious iced.

> 1 inch of fresh lemongrass, thinly sliced, or 1 teaspoon
>   dried lemongrass
> 1 piece of crystallized ginger, about 1 inch (2.5 cm) square
> 250 ml boiling water

Place the sliced lemongrass in a cup. Cut the ginger into smaller pieces and add to the cup. Pour the boiling water over both and steep for 5 minutes. (If you're using dried lemongrass, steep a bit longer, up to 15 minutes, to extract the most flavour.) Strain and serve.

yield:
  1 serving (250 ml)

per serving (estimated):
  13 calories, 0 g protein, 3 g carbohydrates, 0 g fat, 0 mg cholesterol, 0 g dietary fibre, 8 mg sodium.

4

The cold, sparkling cocktails in
this chapter, made with soda
water or naturally sparkling spring
water, range from light, fruity
beverages suitable for an evening
soiree to sweet, soothing drinks
that are perfect for those with an
upset stomach. I've included
some vegetable juice cocktails,
brimming with vitamins and
minerals, as well.

cocktails
and other sparkling beverages

Tomato Cocktail

Made with fortified soya milk, this smooth cocktail contains 4 milligrams of iron – more than one-quarter of the recommended Daily Value for women. The vitamin C in the tomatoes helps our bodies absorb the nonheme (plant-derived) iron they also contain. The healthy fat in olive oil helps us absorb the antioxidant found in tomatoes, lycopene.

225 g stewed tomatoes, canned, no salt.
50 ml plain non-fat yogurt or fortified soya milk
½ teaspoon blackstrap molasses
¼ teaspoon olive oil

Combine all the ingredients in a blender and process until smooth. Serve over ice.

yield:
1 serving (250 ml)

per serving (with yogurt):
117 calories, 5 g protein, 20 g carbohydrates, 1 g fat, 1 mg cholesterol, 4 g dietary fibre, 76 mg sodium. High in vitamin C, calcium, iron, and a good source of dietary fibre, vitamin A, riboflavin, vitamin B^{12}, and potassium.

Orange Ginger Quencher

Keep a jar of the base for this light, refreshing drink in the refrigerator so it's ready to add to soda water on a hot summer day. It's high in healing vitamin C and contains spicy ginger to soothe the stomach. Ginger can be minced using a ginger grater (available in Asian supermarkets) or a garlic press.

> 1 teaspoon minced ginger
> 250 ml boiling water
> 2 teaspoons sugar or honey (or less according to taste)
> 125 ml orange juice
> 250 ml soda water

Place minced ginger in a cup. Pour the boiling water over the ginger and steep for 5 minutes. Strain and pour the ginger tea into a pitcher. Stir in the sugar, add ice, and stir once more. Then add the orange juice and soda water. Stir and serve.

yield:
> 4 servings (125 ml each)

per serving:
> 22 calories, 0.2 g protein, 5 g carbohydrates, 0.1 g fat, 0 mg cholesterol, 0 g dietary fibre, 13 mg sodium. High in vitamin C.

UTI Cocktail

A mixture of baking soda and water is a popular folk remedy for bladder and urinary tract infections. Drink a UTI cocktail and call your doctor at the first signs of a urinary tract or bladder infection (pain and burning when urinating, frequent urination, passing blood, or voiding only small amounts). Don't drink this cocktail on a full stomach or if you're on a low-sodium diet. For additional relief, add baking soda to a bath and soak in it for a few minutes.

½ teaspoon baking soda
250 ml water

Combine the baking soda and water. Serve immediately.

yield:
1 serving (250 ml)

per serving:
0 calories, 0 g protein, 0 g carbohydrates, 0 g dietary fibre, 0 mg cholesterol, 636 mg sodium.

Cranberry Fizz

This sparkling drink is light and delicious. With antioxidant vitamin C and cancer-fighting ellagic acid, cranberry juice is a wonderful immune-system booster. Cranberry juice can help prevent urinary tract infections, too.

250 ml cranberry juice
125 ml sparkling water or soda water
1 teaspoon lemon juice
ice
lemon slice (garnish)

Combine cranberry juice, sparkling water or soda water, and lemon juice in a glass. Stir and add ice and a lemon slice.

yield:
1 serving (300 ml)

per serving:
146 calories, 0 g protein, 37 g carbohydrates, 0.3 g fat, 0 mg cholesterol, 0.3 g dietary fibre, 7 mg sodium. High in vitamin C.

cranberry juice
and cranberry juice cocktail

Check product labels to see how much cranberry juice is in your cranberry juice cocktail. Cranberry juice has to be sweetened to make it palatable. Some cranberry juice cocktails contain only 27 per cent juice, and many others contain even less. Look for a cocktail that lists cranberry juice as the first or second ingredient (often, high-fructose corn syrup will be listed first). If cranberry juice or cocktail is too acidic for your stomach, try diluting it with water.

Frosty Apricot
Mint Cooler

This drink provides 35 per cent of the recommended Daily Value of vitamin A and 50 per cent of the Daily Value of vitamin C. It's low in calories and thirst-quenching, too. Don't forget to eat the mint garnish – it contains anti-cancer compounds.

> 180 ml apricot purée
> 125 ml soda water or sparkling water (no sodium)
> mint garnish

Combine the apricot purée and soda water in a glass. Garnish with mint.

yield:
> 1 serving (300 ml)

per serving:
> 95 calories, 1 g protein, 25 g carbohydrates, 0.2 g fat, 0 mg cholesterol, 1 g dietary fibre, 6 mg sodium. High in vitamin A, carotenoids, and vitamin C (if fortified).

apricots

Choose deep orange-gold apricots without green spots – the darker and brighter they are, the more beta-carotene and other carotenoids they contain. Ripe apricots are firm but give slightly when finger pressure is applied. Apricots can be ripened at home, but once ripe should be stored in the refrigerator.

Fresh apricot purée is delicious, high in dietary fibre, and can be diluted with soda water or sparkling water to suit your taste. To make apricot purée, remove the stones from four to six apricots. Purée the apricots in a blender with 2 to 3 tablespoons of water. Or simply purée 168 g canned, juice-packed apricots along with 2 to 3 tablespoons of their juices.

Blackberry Sparkle

Reach for a Blackberry Sparkle instead of a cola. It's low in calories and contains no artificial sweeteners, caffeine, or sodium. And unlike cola, it's low in phosphates, which can rob your body of calcium. Blackberries provide your body with ellagic acid, which may help prevent cancer.

> 2 tablespoons blackberry syrup (see page 208)
> 175 ml soda water or sparkling water
> ice

Pour the syrup into a glass. Add the soda water and stir. Serve over ice.

yield:

1 serving (175 ml)

per serving:

105 calories, 0 g protein, 26 g carbohydrates, 0 g fat, 0 mg cholesterol, 0 g dietary fibre, 2 mg sodium. High in copper. A good source of vitamin C.

drink to your health

Orange Pineapple Refresher

While your friends are sipping their cocktails, you can sip this non-alcoholic drink. Tropical fruit juices make it high in vitamin C. For a sophisticated touch, serve Orange Pineapple Refresher in an interesting glass with a fresh pineapple triangle.

> 125 ml orange juice
> 73 g pineapple chunks
> 35 g granulated sugar or 2 tablespoons sugar syrup
>   (see page 201)
> 2 tablespoons fresh lemon juice
> 250 ml sparkling water
> Pineapple slices (for garnish)

In a blender combine the orange juice, pineapple chunks, granulated sugar or sugar syrup, and lemon juice. Process until the pineapple is smooth. Divide between two glasses; add 125 ml sparkling water to each and stir. Serve garnished with pineapple slices.

yield:
   2 servings (250 ml each)

per serving:
   148 calories, 1 g protein, 38 g carbohydrates, 0.3 g fat, 0 mg cholesterol, 1 g dietary fibre, 3 mg sodium. High in vitamin C.

Lemon Aid

Drink this one when you have a cold or flu. It's based on an old folk remedy I learned from my friend Luis, who is originally from the Dominican Republic. If you like, add 2 teaspoons of raspberry syrup (see page 211) and try a Raspberry Lemon Aid. Limonene, a phyto-chemical in lemon and citrus fruits, may help our bodies fight cancer.

> 250 ml boiling water
> 3–4 tablespoons freshly squeezed lemon juice or 1 lemon,
>   quartered
> 3 teaspoons honey

Combine boiling water and lemon juice in a cup (or combine cool water and 2 lemon quarters in a mug and microwave for 1.5 minutes; squeeze the juice from the remaining 2 lemon quarters into the mug.) Stir in honey. Serve hot.

yield:
> 1 serving (250 ml)

per serving:
> 76 calories, 0.2 g protein, 21 g carbohydrates, 0 g fat, 0 mg cholesterol, 0.2 g dietary fibre, 8 mg sodium. High in vitamin C.

Note: For Raspberry Lemon Aid add 2 teaspoons of unsweetened Raspberry Syrup (see Staples section page 211) to the Lemon Aid.

per serving:
> 110 calories, 0.2 g protein, 30 g carbohydrates, 0 g fat, 0 mg cholesterol, 0.2 g dietary fibre, 9 mg sodium. High in vitamin C.

Sy's Lime Rickey

My husband, Sy, likes to cool down after a game of tennis with a refreshing Lime Rickey. It's an excellent thirst quencher. When made with fructose and served icy cold, it would also be good for a hangover.

3 tablespoons lime juice
1 tablespoon (12 g) fructose, 1 tablespoon (12 g) sugar or
      3–4 g non-caloric sweetener
250 ml sparkling water, spring water, or soda water
ice
lime wedge or slice (for garnish)

Combine the lime juice and fructose or sweetener in a tall glass. Stir to dissolve. Add the sparkling water, spring water, or soda water. Mix, then add enough ice to fill the glass. Garnish with a lime wedge or slice. Serve.

yield:
  1 serving (250 ml)

per serving:
  57 calories, 0.2 g protein, 16 g carbohydrates, 0 g fat, 0 mg cholesterol, 0.2 g dietary fibre, 4 mg sodium. High in vitamin C.

Quick Comeback

I developed the Quick Comeback for my friends who find tomato juice helpful when nursing a hangover. You don't have to have a hangover to enjoy it: it's low in calories, and high in lycopene and vitamins A and C. Canned vegetable juices can be high in sodium, so make sure you buy low-sodium V-8 for this drink. Nutritional yeast can be added for extra nutrition and flavour.

> 1 small can (175 ml) low-sodium V-8
> ½ teaspoon unsulphured molasses
> 3 tablespoons plain non-fat or low-fat yogurt
> ½ teaspoon nutritional yeast (optional)
> ice

Combine ingredients in a mug or glass. Stir, add ice, and serve.

yield:
   1 serving (250 ml)

per serving:
   74 calories, 4 g protein, 13 g carbohydrates, 0 g fat, 0.8 mg cholesterol, 2 g dietary fibre, 128 mg sodium. High in vitamin A and vitamin C. A good source of thiamine, riboflavin, vitamin B^{12}, folate, calcium, and iron.

Strawberry Wine Cooler

According to the National Institute of Health, moderate alcohol intake (no more than two glasses of wine a day) has been associated with a decreased risk of heart disease and stroke. In moderation (no more than two glasses a day), it can also help lower blood cholesterol. That's reason enough to try this sparkling strawberry cooler.

> 2 tablespoons fresh strawberry juice or 1 tablespoon strawberry syrup
> 50 ml dry red wine
> 125 ml sparkling water or soda water
> ice

Strawberry juice is prepared by juicing whole fresh strawberries. About 4 large strawberries will yield 2 tablespoons of juice. Combine the juice, wine and sparkling water in a glass. Serve over ice.

yield:
> 1 serving (175 ml)

per serving:
> 51 calories, 0.3 g protein, 3 g carbohydrates, 0 g fat, 0 mg cholesterol, 0 g dietary fibre, 4 mg sodium. A good source of vitamin C.

Blackberry Wine Cooler

This wine cooler looks and tastes like a festive holiday punch. Use a blackberry syrup made from real berries and sugar (see page 208) to get the health benefits of berries. Red wine and berries both contain ellagic acid, a cancer-fighting flavonoid.

> 1 tablespoon blackberry syrup
> 2 tablespoons water
> 50 ml dry red wine
> 50 ml sparkling water

Combine ingredients and serve over ice.

yield:
   1 serving (125 ml)

per serving:
   52 calories, 0 g protein, 3 g carbohydrates, 0 g fat, 0 mg cholesterol, 0.3 g dietary fibre, 7 mg sodium.

drink to your health

Tummy Rescue Remedy

Sweet, soothing, and perfect for relieving the symptoms of stomach flu. Ginger soothes the digestive system, while cranberry juice adds phytochemicals and vitamin C to strengthen the immune system.

> 2 tablespoons homemade ginger syrup (see p. 202)
> 150 ml bottled cranberry juice cocktail

Combine the ginger syrup and cranberry juice cocktail in a glass. Serve over ice.

yield:
> 1 serving (150 ml)

per serving:
> 99 calories, 0 g protein, 25 g carbohydrates, 0 g fat, 0 mg cholesterol, 0 g dietary fibre, 4 mg sodium. High in vitamin C.

Homemade Ginger Ale

Making your own ginger ale is easy when you keep ginger syrup on hand. It contains fewer calories and more real ginger than you'll find in commercial ginger ales. I find it tastes better, too!

50 ml ginger syrup (see page 202)
50 ml soda water
ice
1 slice of lemon or lime (for garnish)

Pour the syrup into a glass and add the soda water. Stir. Add ice and slice of lemon or lime. Serve.

yield:
1 serving (175 ml)

per serving:
34 calories, 0.3 g protein, 8 g carbohydrates, 0 g fat, 0 mg cholesterol, 0.3 g dietary fibre, 7 mg sodium.

Orangeberry Lift

One serving of Orangeberry Lift provides 71 milligrams of vitamin C – more than 100 per cent of the recommended Daily Value. And because it's made with blueberries, this drink can help slow ageing and prevent cancer too.

> 73 g blueberries
> 125 ml orange juice
> 2 tablespoons low-fat or skimmed-milk or soya milk
> 125 ml sparkling water or soda water

Combine the blueberries, orange juice and milk in the blender. Purée. Pour into a glass. Add the sparkling water or soda water and stir. Serve.

yield:
> 1 serving (375 ml)

per serving with low-fat milk:
> 152 calories, 3 g protein, 36 g carbohydrates, 1 g fat, 2 mg cholesterol, 2 g dietary fibre, 27 mg sodium. High in vitamin C and folate. A good source of carbohydrates, dietary fibre, vitamin A, thiamine, vitamin E, and potassium.

Fresh Mint Tinkle

I found a recipe for Fresh Mint Tinkle in a box of my mother's old recipes. It appeared in an article about 'good tasting cold drinks' in the magazine *American Weekly* on July 1, 1951. I modified the recipe but kept its oh-so-1950s name. My version is good tasting *and* good for you, with 65 per cent of the recommended Daily Value of vitamin C.

    125 ml water
    100 g granulated sugar
    20 mint leaves, chopped
    125 ml fresh lime juice
    300 ml red grapefruit juice
    500 ml soda water or sparkling water
    ice

Start by making a sweet mint syrup. Combine the water and sugar in a pot and heat until simmering. Simmer for about 5 minutes or until all the sugar has dissolved. Add the chopped mint and let steep for 10 minutes or until cool. Strain the syrup, then combine it with the lime juice and grapefruit juice in a large pitcher. Add the soda water and stir. Serve over ice.

The mint syrup can also be refrigerated and used to prepare one serving at a time. For one glass of Fresh Mint Tinkle, combine 50 ml of mint syrup with 2 tablespoons of lime juice, 5 tablespoons of grapefruit juice, 125 ml of soda water. Serve over ice.

Note that because the tart juices used here require extra sweetener, the mint syrup in this recipe contains more sugar than does the mint syrup that appears in the Staples section of this book (page 204).

drink to your health

yield:

4 servings (250 ml each)

per serving:

136 calories, 1 g protein, 35 g carbohydrates, 0 g fat, 0 mg cholesterol, 0.3 g dietary fibre, 149 mg sodium. High in vitamin C.

Persimmon
Pineapple Pleasure

I love the astringent taste of persimmon. Combined with the tropical pineapple juice, it makes a delicious and nutrient-rich, high-fibre cocktail. Look for Japanese persimmon, which are sweet and large.

For a Creamy Persimmon Pineapple Pleasure omit the sparkling water and add 50 ml plain non-fat yogurt and 100 ml skimmed milk.

    1 large, ripe persimmon
    125 ml pineapple juice, canned or fresh
    125 ml sparkling water

Wash the persimmon well and remove the stem. Cut the fruit into eighths and place in a blender. Add the pineapple juice and purée. Pour into a large glass. Add the sparkling water and stir. Serve plain or with ice.

yield:

    1 serving (250 ml)

per serving:

    188 calories, 1 g protein, 49 g carbohydrates, 0.4 g fat, 0 mg cholesterol, 6 g dietary fibre, 4 mg sodium. High in dietary fibre, vitamin A, vitamin C, and folate. A good source of thiamine, vitamin B^6, vitamin E, copper, magnesium, and potassium.

drink to your health

per serving with yogurt and milk (400 ml):

265 calories, 9 g protein, 59 g carbohydrates, 6 g dietary fibre, 1 g fat, 3 mg cholesterol, 113 mg sodium. High in vitamin A, riboflavin, vitamin B^{12}, vitamin C, vitamin D, dietary fibre, folate, calcium, magnesium and potassium. A good source of protein, thiamine, vitamin E, copper, selenium and zinc.

persimmon

Autumn is the season for persimmon, a fruit with tomato-like colour and skin that is grown in Japan, China, Florida, and southern France. Wash the fruit well to clean the skin, which is edible, and enjoy persimmon raw or cooked. A ripe persimmon will feel like a ripe tomato; it will yield slightly when light finger pressure is applied to its surface.

Papaya Zinger

This sparkling, tropical drink delivers 225 per cent of the recommended Daily Value for vitamin C. Use coconut extract for that familiar island flavour without additional calories or fat.

    ½ papaya, peeled, seeded, and puréed or 150 ml fresh or
        bottled papaya purée
    75 ml orange juice
    75 ml sparkling water
    fructose to taste
    few drops coconut extract
    ice
    mint leaf and slice of fresh coconut (for garnish)

Combine the papaya purée, orange juice, and coconut extract. Stir well. Add the sparkling water and stir again. Serve over ice, with a garnish of mint leaf and fresh coconut wedge.

yield:
   1 serving (325 ml)

per serving:
   96 calories, 2 g protein, 23 g carbohydrates, 0.4 g fat, 0 mg cholesterol, 3 g dietary fibre, 6 mg sodium. High in vitamin C, vitamin E, and folate. A good source of dietary fibre, vitamin A, thiamine, and potassium.

Leanne's Orange Passion

My daughter Leanne lived and worked in the Dominican Republic and Mexico, where she learned to love the native fruits. Together we developed this immune-system boosting drink. Leanne suggests using champagne instead of sparkling water.

½ passion fruit
3 tablespoons orange juice
1 tablespoon frozen vanilla yogurt
¾ teaspoon fructose (or sugar or other preferred
        sweetener)
125 ml sparkling water or soda water
ice

Combine the passion fruit, orange juice, and vanilla frozen yogurt in a blender and process until smooth. Pour into a tall glass. Add the fructose and stir. Add the sparkling water or soda water. Stir and serve over ice.

yield:
1 serving (175 ml)

per serving:
61 calories, 2 g protein, 13 g carbohydrates, 1 g fat, 6 mg cholesterol, 1 g dietary fibre, 11 mg sodium. High in vitamin C.

passion
fruit

Passion fruit has a thick, tough skin that is purple when ripe. Cut one in half to reveal a fleshy, golden-coloured mass scattered with tiny black seeds. The flesh can be used in fruit salads and, of course, in beverage recipes like this one. The seeds are edible, too; strain them out or let them fall to the bottom of your glass.

5

Vegetables make hot soups and broths excellent sources of nutrients and dietary fibre. The soups in this chapter are designed to be puréed and sipped from a mug or thermos. Many make perfect meals-on-the-go (and soothing, healthful snacks for those stuck home in bed).

Creamy Shiitake Broth

Easy to prepare in the microwave and low in calories and fat, this hot broth carries a lot of nutritional weight. Garlic and mushrooms, particularly shiitake, enhance the immune system and may have cancer-fighting properties. Garlic also contains allicin, a natural antibiotic. And, thanks to the vegetables, miso, and soya milk, this broth is loaded with phytochemicals. Serve it immediately or purée before serving.

175 ml water
23 g chopped shiitake mushrooms (no stems)
23 g chopped white mushrooms
1 teaspoon chopped white or red onion
½ clove garlic, minced
1 teaspoon red miso paste
2 tablespoons soya milk

Combine all the ingredients except the miso and soya milk in a microwave-safe glass measure or bowl. Microwave at high power for 2½ minutes, stirring once about halfway through cooking. Cool slightly (the broth will be very hot when it comes out of the microwave), add the miso and soya milk, then pour into blender and purée. (If you use finely chopped vegetables, you may find you can easily drink this soup without puréeing it.)

yield:
    1 serving (300 ml)

per serving (300 ml):

50 calories, 4 g protein, 7 g carbohydrates, 1 g fat, 0 mg cholesterol, 1 g dietary fibre, 234 mg sodium. A good source of vitamin B^{12}, vitamin D, niacin, riboflavin, and pantothenic acid.

Tomato Veggie Powerhouse

Although preparing it requires a little effort, you can't beat the healing power of the Tomato Veggie Powerhouse. The tomato base is high in lycopene, the antioxidant that helps prevent prostate and other cancers. Vegetables provide fibre, minerals, and loads of healthy phytochemicals. Experiment by adding your favourite vegetables.

1 tablespoon olive oil
1 clove garlic, minced
67 g chopped onions
130 g chopped carrots
750 ml water
320 g shredded cabbage or bok choy
1.350–1.800 kg tomatoes, peeled and chopped
1 turnip, cubed
382 g canned white beans or white kidney beans
123 g dry macaroni
182 g frozen mixed vegetables
1 teaspoon basil leaves
1 teaspoon thyme leaves
¼ teaspoon black pepper
3 teaspoons red miso paste
625 ml fortified soya milk
3 tablespoons chopped fresh parsley

Heat the oil in a large saucepan. Add the garlic, onions, and carrots, and sauté until the onions are softened. Add the cabbage, tomato, turnip, canned beans, dry macaroni, frozen vegetables, basil, thyme, and black pepper. Cook covered for 15 minutes or until the macaroni and turnip are tender. Combine the miso and the soya milk, add to the soup and heat through. Serve topped with fresh chopped parsley.

yield:

10 servings (500 ml each)

per serving:

216 calories, 11 g protein, 38 g carbohydrates, 4 g fat, 0 mg cholesterol, 6 g dietary fibre, 145 mg sodium. High in protein, dietary fibre, vitamin A, vitamin B^6, vitamin B^{12}, vitamin C, vitamin E, folate, iron, lycopene, magnesium, thiamine, and potassium. A good source of carbohydrates, calcium, copper, niacin, riboflavin, selenium, and zinc.

quick tomato veggie powerhouse

If you're in a real hurry, try the fast-food version of the Tomato Veggie Powerhouse: open a can of ready-to-eat, low-sodium tomato vegetable soup, microwave it in a safe container, then purée it and drink it down. The homemade version has a fresher taste, less sodium, and the added benefits of soya, but canned soup will do if you're in a rush.

drink to your health

Savoury Almond Vegetable Soup

Serve this savoury soup hot or cold, as an appetizer or a mid-morning or mid-afternoon pick-me-up. It's a great drink for blood pressure control and for healing – almonds contain phytochemicals and monounsaturated fat that can strengthen your immune system. You can also mix the chopped almonds and wheat germ and use them as a topping. This soup is based on a recipe from the Almond Board of California.

38 g almonds
1 tablespoon olive oil
1 onion, chopped
75 g chopped celery
½ sweet green pepper, chopped
4 garlic cloves, minced
1 litre fat-free chicken broth
1 tomato, chopped
125 ml medium white wine
1 teaspoon dried basil or 1 tablespoon fresh
½ teaspoon dried oregano or 2 teaspoons fresh
⅛ teaspoon black pepper
175 ml fortified soya milk
4 teaspoons wheat germ

Toast the almonds in a heavy saucepan. Add toasted almonds to the blender and process until they are finely chopped.

Heat the olive oil in a saucepan. Add the onion, celery, green pepper, and garlic, and sauté until tender (about 5 minutes). Add the chicken broth, tomato, wine, basil, oregano and pepper. Heat. Finally, add the soya milk and wheat germ and heat through.

Pour the soup into the blender, add the toasted almonds, and purée until smooth. Serve.

yield:

6 servings (300 ml each)

per serving:

132 calories, 8 g protein, 8 g carbohydrates, 6 g fat, 0 mg cholesterol, 2 g dietary fibre, 140 mg sodium. High in vitamin C and vitamin E. A good source of protein, vitamin A, calcium, folate, iron, magnesium, and potassium.

Homemade Beetroot Borscht

Borscht, a beetroot soup of Russian heritage, is traditionally served hot or cold with sour cream, but yogurt makes a healthy substitute. Blackstrap molasses adds flavour and is an excellent source of iron. With bits of shredded beetroot, this soup is a good source of fibre. For a smoother beverage, strain the soup before serving, or purée the cooked beetroot rather than shredding them.

> 1 kg whole red beetroot
> 1.120 litres water
> 4 tomatoes (peeled, seeded and chopped)
> 1 large onion, quartered
> 2 bay leaves
> 50 ml lemon juice
> 3½ tablespoons blackstrap molasses
> 6 tablespoons plain yogurt or low-fat sour cream (optional)
> brown sugar to taste (optional)

Clean and wash the beetroot, then place them with the water in a large saucepan. Bring to a boil, then cover, lower heat, and cook about 45 minutes or until the beetroot is tender. Remove them from the pan and save the liquid.

Measure the beetroot-cooking liquid and add enough water to make 1.5 l. Peel and shred or finely chop the beetroot. Add them to the cooking liquid with the tomatoes, onion, bay leaves, lemon juice and blackstrap molasses.

Bring the liquid to a boil, lower heat, cover and cook for 20 minutes. Remove the onion and bay leaves. Add brown sugar for sweetness if desired. Serve warm, or chill and serve cold with yogurt or sour cream.

yield:

6–8 servings (375 ml each)

per serving:

99 calories, 3 g protein, 23 g carbohydrates, 1 g fat, 0 mg cholesterol, 4 g dietary fibre, 117 mg sodium. High in vitamin C, folate, iron, magnesium, and potassium. A good source of dietary fibre, vitamin A, vitamin B^6, calcium, and copper.

Apple Parsnip Power

Sweet and savoury Apple Parsnip Power is so delicious you won't believe it's healthy, too. Flavonoids (from the apples and apple juice) and folate (from the parsnips) together provide protection from arteriosclerosis. Nutrient-dense and high in fibre, this soup makes a fine meal.

    2 teaspoons canola (rapeseed) oil
    ½ medium onion, chopped
    375 ml fat-free chicken broth
    ¼ teaspoon ground coriander
    ⅛ teaspoon cardamom
    1 large apple, peeled and chunked (225 g)
    2 parsnips, peeled and chunked (225 g)
    125 ml apple juice
    2 tablespoons plain non-fat yogurt

Heat the oil in a small saucepan, add the chopped onion and sauté for a few minutes until the onion softens. Add the chicken broth, coriander, and cardamom and bring to the boil. Then add the apple and parsnip and when the mixture is boiling again, lower the heat to simmer, cover and cook for 20 minutes until the parsnips are tender. Cool slightly. Pour the mixture into a blender and purée. Add the apple juice to thin the soup to the preferred consistency. Add a tablespoon of yogurt before serving.

yield:
2 servings (250 ml each)

per serving:

250 calories, 8 g protein, 45 g carbohydrates, 5 g fat, 0.3 mg cholesterol, 7 g dietary fibre, 154 mg sodium. High in dietary fibre, vitamin C, folate, and potassium. A good source of protein, carbohydrates, vitamin B^6, calcium, copper, iron, niacin, thiamine, magnesium, and phosphorus.

drink to your health

Mug o'Barley

Try this quick and easy hot drink for breakfast. It's high in soluble fibre, so it helps keep cholesterol down and can prevent diverticulosis. You'll find barley flakes (a pre-cooked, dried and flattened form of barley) in health food shops, or look for 'quick barley' near the oatmeal in your supermarket. If you have more time to cook, use pearl barley in this recipe – you'll double its dietary fibre content.

> 250 ml water (or 375 ml if using pearl barley)
> 30 g barley flakes (or 48 g pearl barley)
> lemon wedge
> ½ teaspoon sugar or to taste
> milk to taste

Combine the 250 ml water, the barley flakes and the lemon wedge in a small saucepan. Bring to a boil, lower the heat and simmer for 8 minutes. (For pearl barley, use 375 ml of water and simmer for 30 minutes or until tender.) Remove the lemon wedge. Combine the barley and liquid in a blender and purée until smooth. Pour into a mug. Add sugar or milk to taste.

yield:
   1 serving (250 ml)

per serving:
   91 calories, 3 g protein, 23 g carbohydrates, 1 g fat, 0 mg cholesterol, 4 g dietary fibre, 7 mg sodium. A good source of dietary fibre.

Pumpkin Apple Healer

Delicious in autumn or any time of year, this creamy orange soup is high in healing vitamin A and beta carotene. It's an excellent choice for those with fibromyalgia because it contains both malic acid (in the apple juice) and magnesium (in the pumpkin).

> 1 teaspoon olive oil
> 45 g chopped onions
> 500 ml puréed or canned pumpkin (425 g can)
> 375 ml apple cider or apple juice
> 125 ml fat-free chicken broth
> ½ teaspoon minced ginger
> ¼ teaspoon cinnamon
> 125 ml silken tofu or soya milk
> 50 ml low-fat sour cream or yogurt (optional) for garnish

Heat the oil in a saucepan. Add the chopped onions and sauté for 10 minutes until softened. Add the pumpkin, apple juice, chicken broth, ginger and cinnamon. Simmer for about 10 minutes. Cool slightly and combine in blender with the tofu or soya milk. Purée. Serve warm with a dollop of sour cream or yogurt. Can also be served cold.

yield:

4 servings (250 ml each)

per serving:

121 calories, 4 g protein, 23 g carbohydrates, 3 g fat, 0 mg cholesterol, 4 g dietary fibre, 32 mg sodium. High in vitamin A. A good source of vitamin C, copper, iron, magnesium, and potassium.

fresh
pumpkin purée

To make fresh pumpkin purée, cut a pumpkin in half and remove the seeds and fibres. Place the halves cut-side down on a baking sheet and bake in a 400°F (200°C, gas mark 6) oven until tender, about 40 minutes. Cool slightly, then remove the skin and cut the pumpkin into chunks. Use a food processor or blender to purée.

If you have a microwave, you can place the pumpkin half cut-side down on a microwave-safe plate or pie plate. Use a fork to pierce the skin a few times, and microwave on high for 4 minutes to soften the skin, which can then be easily removed. Let stand 3 minutes. Remove skin. Cut into cubes. Place in microwave safe container, cover and microwave on HIGH for 4–5 minutes, then purée.

The pumpkin can be boiled to soften for puréeing. Cut the pumpkin in half; remove the seeds and stringy part. Cube the pumpkin with the skin on. Place in a saucepan with water to cover. Bring the water to a boil, lower the heat, cover, and cook until tender, about 15–30 minutes. Peel and purée.

Hot Garlic, Carrot, and Broccoli Soup

Here's a full-flavoured, savoury soup that will boost your immune system — another great choice for a cold, flu, or sore throat. Garlic and onion have antibacterial properties, and cayenne or hot sauce will relieve congestion and clear the sinuses.

1 tablespoon olive oil
1 medium onion, chopped
4 cloves garlic, minced
1 carrot, peeled and sliced
500 ml chicken stock, chicken broth, or Jewish Penicillin
    (see page 160)
352 g washed, peeled and cut broccoli
1 tomato, chopped
2 tablespoons chopped parsley
110 g spinach or kale, washed
dash of black pepper and cayenne pepper
hot sauce (optional)

Heat the olive oil in a large saucepan. Add the onion, carrot and garlic, and sauté for 5 to 10 minutes or until the onions are tender. Add the chicken stock, broccoli, kale (if you are using it), tomato, and parsley. Bring to a boil then lower heat, cover, and cook for 15 to 20 minutes or until the broccoli is tender. Add the spinach. Continue to cook uncovered for 2 minutes. Allow to cool, then purée. Pour the soup back into the pot and stir in the black pepper and cayenne pepper. Serve. Pass the hot sauce!

yield:

4–6 servings (375 ml each)

per cup serving (estimated) with spinach:

109 calories, 7 g protein, 13 g carbohydrates, 4 g fat, 0 mg cholesterol, 5 g dietary fibre, 149 mg sodium. High in vitamin C, vitamin A, and folate. A good source of protein, dietary fibre, vitamin B^6, vitamin E, calcium, iron, magnesium, niacin, riboflavin, and potassium.

Tomato Pumpkin Soup

Topped with a dollop of non-fat or light yogurt or sour cream and some chopped parsley, this delicious soup is a splendid beginning to a festive meal. Pumpkins are high in beta carotene and fibre; they also contain iron, vitamin C and complex carbohydrates. And, of course, they add glorious colour.

    1 tablespoon olive oil
    1 medium onion, finely chopped
    1 stalk celery, finely chopped
    1 carrot, finely chopped
    375 ml canned or puréed pumpkin (see p. 155)
    1 (415 g) can stewed no salt added tomatoes
    500 ml water
    1 teaspoon sugar
    ¼ teaspoon ground nutmeg
    black pepper to taste
    50 ml non-fat plain yogurt (for garnish)
    2 tablespoons chopped parsley (for garnish)

Heat the oil in a large saucepan. Add the onion, celery and carrot and sauté for 10 minutes or until softened. Add the pumpkin, tomatoes and water. Bring to a boil, lower heat, cover and cook for 10–15 minutes or until flavours blend. Remove half of the soup and transfer it to a blender or food processor. Purée until smooth. Remove and purée the other half. Pour the soup back into the saucepan. Add the sugar and ground nutmeg. Reheat for about five minutes and add pepper to taste. Serve, garnished with a dollop of yogurt and some chopped parsley.

drink to your health

yield:

6 servings (250 ml each)

per serving:

83 calories, 2 g protein, 14 g carbohydrates, 3 g fat, 0 mg cholesterol, 4 g dietary fibre, 31 mg sodium. High in vitamin A and vitamin C. A good source of vitamin E, folate, and iron.

Jewish Penicillin

Jewish mothers have long recognized the healing powers of hot chicken soup. The garlic and cayenne pepper in this recipe add extra healing power and help relieve congestion. Use the entire onion, including its peel, for a lovely, golden-coloured broth. Add cayenne pepper or hot sauce, whatever makes you sweat!

Jewish Penicillin can be used in any recipe that calls for chicken stock. You can also freeze one-cup portions and use them for emergencies. Quickly thaw the individual portions in a pot or in the microwave and add frozen vegetables, cooked rice, or pasta.

1.8 kg raw chicken (wings or legs are fine)
3 litres water
1 onion, quartered and unpeeled
12 sprigs parsley
2 stalks celery, cut into ¾-inch lengths
4 carrots, scrubbed and cut into ¾-inch lengths
2 bay leaves
3 cloves garlic, sliced
¼ teaspoon black pepper, cayenne pepper, or hot sauce

In a large soup pot, add the chicken and water and bring to a boil. Skim off the surface froth. Lower heat and add the onion, parsley, celery, carrots and bay leaves. Cover and cook for about an hour. Remove from heat. Allow to cool slightly. Strain and add pepper, cayenne pepper, or hot sauce to taste.

If desired, refrigerate stock and remove fat then reheat before serving.

yield:

8 servings (250 ml each)

per cup (estimated):

179 calories, 26 mg protein, 6 g carbohydrates, 5 g fat, 81 mg cholesterol, 0 g fibre, 106 mg sodium. High in protein, vitamin A, and zinc. A good source of potassium.

quick chicken stock

If you're using cartons or cans of chicken broth or soup, check to make sure the first ingredient on the label is chicken or chicken broth. And look for a brand that is low in sodium – less than 500 mg per serving.

Manhattan Clam Chowder

This tomato and clam chowder is hearty and healthy. Clams provide vitamin B^{12}, copper, and healthy omega-3 fatty acids, while tomatoes and potatoes deliver immune-enhancing glutathione. Onions and garlic add an extra immune system boost. You'll need a spoon for this one.

- 1 tablespoon olive oil
- 67 g chopped onion
- 75 g chopped celery
- 2 cloves garlic, minced or sliced
- 326 g cubed potato
- 1 (275 g) can clams with liquid or 1 pint fresh clams and liquid
- 125 ml water
- 2–3 tablespoons chopped fresh parsley
- 1 teaspoon dried thyme
- 324 g chopped peeled and seeded tomatoes
- dash sugar and ground black pepper

Heat the oil in a medium saucepan. Add the onion, celery, and garlic and sauté for about 5 minutes or until softened. Drain the liquid from the clams (about 175 ml) and add it to the saucepan along with the water, reserving the clams for later use. Bring to a boil. Add the potatoes, 2 tablespoons of the parsley, and thyme and cook over medium heat until the potatoes are tender, about 8 minutes. Add the reserved clams (or fresh clams and liquid) and the tomatoes and heat through. Finally, add the sugar, pepper, additional parsley, and water if necessary. Serve.

drink to your health

yield:

4–6 servings (about 250 ml each)

per serving:

131 calories, 3 g protein, 23 g carbohydrates, 4 g fat, 2 mg cholesterol, 3 g dietary fibre, 180 mg sodium. High in vitamin B^{12}, vitamin C, and copper. A good source of dietary fibre, vitamin A, vitamin B^6, magnesium, potassium, and thiamine.

Creamy Split Pea Soup

Thick and creamy, this soup is high in protein and very high in fibre, with 16 grams per serving. If that's too much fibre for you, try thinning the soup with chicken or vegetable broth. You'll get a delicious vegetarian soup if you use vegetable stock (see page 212) instead of water and omit the chicken.

> 1.750 litres water, or 1.750 litres vegetable stock for
>   vegetarian soup
> 450 g chicken legs (4 drumsticks), skin removed (omit for
>   vegetarian version)
> 137 g chopped carrots
> 135 g chopped onions
> 400 g split peas
> 1 clove garlic, minced
> ½ teaspoon oregano
> ¼ teaspoon thyme
> dash pepper

Combine the water and chicken in a large soup saucepan. Bring to a boil and skim the foam. Lower the heat and add the remaining ingredients. Cover and cook for 45 minutes. Remove the chicken. Purée the remaining soup in batches in a blender or food processor.

yield:
   8 servings (250 ml each)

per serving:

270 calories, 22 g protein, 42 g carbohydrates, 2 g fat, 20 mg cholesterol, 16 g dietary fibre, 34 mg sodium. High in protein, dietary fibre, vitamin A, folate, magnesium, potassium, and zinc. A good source of carbohydrates, copper, iron, selenium.

Phyto-Favourite

Served hot or cold, the Phyto-Favourite will boost your immune system. The garlic, onions, watercress, and tomato contain lots of healing phytochemicals. Drink it hot if you're suffering from a cold or flu.

1½ teaspoons olive oil
1 clove garlic, minced
135 g chopped onions
500 ml fat-free chicken broth
2 tablespoons short-grain white rice
1 bunch watercress, about 135 g
125 ml plain skimmed yogurt
2 tablespoons chopped tomato (for garnish)

Heat the oil in a saucepan. Add the garlic and onions and sauté on low for about 10 minutes until the onions are softened. Add the chicken broth and white rice and bring to a boil. Lower the heat, cover and cook for 15 minutes. Meanwhile, wash and drain the watercress, remove the thicker stems, and coarsely chop the remaining watercress.

Add the watercress and continue to cook for 5 more minutes. Combine all the ingredients in a blender and purée. Then add the yogurt and purée again. Serve immediately or chill. Garnish with chopped tomato.

yield:

4 servings (175 ml each)

drink to your health

per serving:

92 calories, 7 g protein, 12 g carbohydrates, 2 g fat, 0.6 mg cholesterol, 1.4 g dietary fibre, 124 mg sodium. High in vitamin A, vitamin C, and beta carotene. A good source of protein, calcium, and potassium.

My Best Gazpacho

Gazpacho is a spicy, cold Spanish soup made with chopped summer vegetables. My version is healthy and without added oil, and with avocado for added protein, monounsaturated oils, and potassium. Of course, with all the vegetables, it's high in fibre and packed with phytochemicals, too.

> 1 large tomato, quartered
> 35 g cubed avocado
> 2 tablespoons chopped green onion
> 2 tablespoons chopped sweet green pepper
> 1 teaspoon Worcestershire sauce
> dash salt and pepper
> dash hot sauce

Combine the ingredients in the blender and purée. More hot pepper sauce can be added for taste.

yield:

1 serving (250 ml)

per serving:

111 calories, 3 g protein, 14 g carbohydrates, 6 g fat, 0 mg cholesterol, 5 g dietary fibre, 78 mg sodium. High in vitamin A, vitamin C, and potassium. A good source of dietary fibre, vitamin B^6, copper, folate, niacin, iron, magnesium, and thiamine.

Oyster Stew

Canned oysters make this stew quick and easy. Check labels and buy oysters with the lowest sodium content you can find. Alternatively, you can prepare this with fresh oysters. In a quick low-fat and low-calorie soup, oysters provide iron, omega-3 fatty acids, vitamin B^{12} and zinc.

1 teaspoon olive oil
2 tablespoons finely chopped onion
2 tablespoons finely chopped celery, including leaves
1 can (225 g) whole oysters
250 ml semi-skimmed milk or soya milk
¼ teaspoon Worcestershire sauce

Heat the olive oil in a small pan. Add the onion and celery and sauté until softened, 5 or more minutes. Combine the liquid from the oyster can, the milk, and the Worcestershire sauce in the pan and heat slowly. Cut the oysters into bite size pieces and add to the pan. Continue to heat about 2 or 3 minutes until hot. Serve.

To prepare with fresh oysters, use about a dozen fresh oysters, reserving the liquid. When the onions and celery are softened, add the oysters and sauté until the edges are curling and slightly darkened, and then add the remaining ingredients and enough reserved liquid to make it the consistency you prefer.

yield:
  2 servings (250 ml each)

per serving:

160 calories, 12 g protein, 11 g carbohydrates, 7 g fat, 3 g mono-fat, 2 g saturated fat, 71 mg cholesterol, 0.3 g dietary fibre, 197 mg sodium. High in protein, vitamin B^{12}, vitamin D, copper, iron, calcium, magnesium, riboflavin, selenium, and zinc. Good source of vitamin A, vitamin C, thiamine, and potassium.

Souper Miso

Although it's made from soya, which can help protect our bodies from heart disease and cancer and relieve the symptoms of menopause, miso is very high in sodium. A cup of Souper Miso can be so calming, however, that I've decided to include it here. Try it when you need to relax, or between meals for a caffeine-free beverage.

> 250 ml boiling water, slightly cooled
> 1 teaspoon red miso paste or red soya paste
> tiny cubes of firm tofu (for garnish)

Combine the water and miso paste and stir until the miso is dissolved. Drink while hot, garnished with tiny tofu cubes.

yield:
1 serving (250 ml)

per serving:
10 calories, 1 g protein, 1 g carbohydrates, 0 g fat, 0 mg cholesterol, 0.2 g dietary fibre, 214 mg sodium.

6

The drinks in this chapter, made
with low-fat or non-fat dairy, soya,
or rice milks, make wonderful
snacks or dessert beverages.
Frothy or smooth, milks are
generally easy on the digestive
system. Fruit and vegetable juices
add flavour and nutritional
benefits.

Orange Creamsicle Shake

This creamy shake will remind you of the popular orange-vanilla ice cream treats you enjoyed as a kid. Packed with nutrients and high in calories, fibre, protein, and carbohydrates, it makes an excellent breakfast substitute. Cut the recipe in half if you'd prefer a lower-calorie beverage.

375 ml vanilla frozen yogurt, non-fat, low-fat, or regular
125 ml skimmed milk (or your choice)
1 banana, cut into thick slices
3 tablespoons frozen orange juice concentrate
2 teaspoons dry egg-white powder

Combine all ingredients in a blender and purée.

yield:
1 serving (325 ml)

per serving with non-fat frozen yogurt and skimmed milk:
564 calories, 20 g protein, 118 g carbohydrates, 2 g fat, 8 mg cholesterol, 3 g dietary fibre, 335 mg sodium. High in protein, carbohydrates, vitamin B^6, vitamin C, folate, calcium, potassium. A good source of dietary fibre, vitamin A, thiamine, riboflavin, vitamin D, copper, iron, magnesium, and selenium.

Calming Almond Milk

In the Ayurvedic healing tradition of India, a glass of warm almond milk is believed to lower anxiety. This high-protein, low-carbohydrate drink is also a good source of vitamin D and calcium, which help to prevent osteoporosis and build strong bones. The calcium, magnesium, and potassium are good for lowering blood pressure. You can strain this milk if you like, but you'll be losing the benefits of the fibre and some of the nutrients.

> 2 tablespoons whole almonds
> 250 ml low-fat or reduced fat or whole milk

Soak the almonds in water (just enough to cover them) overnight. Strain and remove the skins, then purée or finely chop the almonds in a blender. Warm the milk, add it to the blender, and purée. Serve warm.

yield:
1 serving (250 ml)

per serving (with low-fat milk):
219 calories, 13 g protein, 16 g carbohydrates, 12 g fat, 1.5 g saturated fat, 15 mg cholesterol, 2.3 g dietary fibre, 130 mg sodium. High in protein, vitamin D, and calcium. A good source of dietary fibre, vitamin A, magnesium, and potassium.

Tang-Tang

Cranberry and pineapple juices provide vitamin C, healing phyto-chemicals, and lots of tangy taste to this dairy-free drink. Double or triple the recipe and store Tang-Tang in the refrigerator so it's ready when you are. Use the Rice Cure recipe (see page 181) for homemade rice milk (shop-bought works fine, too), or substitute yogurt for the rice milk if you're so inclined.

> 75 ml cranberry juice cocktail
> 75 ml pineapple juice
> 50 ml rice milk

Combine the ingredients in a glass. Add ice and serve.

yield:
　1 serving (about 250 ml)

per serving (with rice milk):
　119 calories, 0.3 g protein, 30 g carbohydrates, 0.2 g fat, 0 mg cholesterol, 0.3 g dietary fibre, 4 mg sodium. High in vitamin C.

Orange Froth

This frothy drink is an excellent source of isoflavones (from the soya) and limonenes (from the citrus), both of which help prevent cancer. The orange juice also provides the antioxidant vitamin C, which promotes a healthy immune system.

Dried egg white adds protein and creates froth, but this drink is delicious without the egg white if it's not available. (Never use fresh raw egg whites, which can carry dangerous bacteria, in this or other beverages.)

175 ml freshly squeezed orange juice
125 ml soya milk or vanilla-flavoured fortified soya milk
1 teaspoon dried egg white
½ teaspoon vanilla extract (optional, not needed if vanilla-flavoured soya milk is used)
ice

Combine ingredients in a blender and process until frothy. Serve over ice.

yield:

1 serving.

per serving with fortified vanilla-flavoured soya milk:

167 calories, 6 g protein, 31 g carbohydrates, 2 g fat, 0 mg cholesterol, 0.4 g dietary fibre, 75 mg sodium. High in vitamin A, vitamin B^{12}, vitamin C, and a good source of protein, carbohydrates, thiamine, vitamin E, folate, calcium, magnesium, and potassium.

Raspberry Rumble

Dairy milk can help lower cholesterol and blood pressure, especially in men. Lower cholesterol levels reduce the risk of heart disease, as do the fibre and vitamin C in this sweet pink drink.

> 61 g fresh or 125 g frozen unsweetened raspberries
> 125 ml skimmed milk or soya milk
> ¼ teaspoon sugar (optional)

Combine the ingredients in a blender and process until smooth. The sugar is optional but does sweeten the milk nicely. Strain the milk before drinking it if you don't like all those raspberry seeds.

yield:
> 1 serving (250 ml)

per serving (unstrained) with skimmed milk:
> 81 calories, 5 g protein, 13 g carbohydrates, 2 g fat, 5 mg cholesterol, 4 g dietary fibre, 62 mg sodium. High in dietary fibre, riboflavin, vitamin B[12], vitamin C, vitamin D, and calcium. A good source of vitamin A, folate, magnesium, manganese, and phosphorus.

New-Fashioned Vanilla Milk Shake

Old-fashioned milk shakes are laden with fat. This smooth, 'new-fashioned' shake, made with non-fat and low-fat dairy products, is a wonderful, much healthier substitute. It's high in carbohydrates, protein, and calcium – a great choice for any time of the day. Go ahead and treat yourself.

> 375 ml non-fat frozen vanilla yogurt
> 125 ml skimmed milk

Combine ingredients in a milkshake machine or blender. Blend and serve.

yield:
   1 serving (about 325 ml)

per serving:
   343 calories, 13 g protein, 69 g carbohydrates, 0.2 g fat, 2 mg cholesterol, 0 g dietary fibre, 273 mg sodium. High in carbohydrates, calcium, protein. A good source of riboflavin, vitamin D, and iron.

drink to your health

The Rice Cure

Bland and easy to digest, rice is often recommended for stomach problems and when recovering from diarrhoea. The Rice Cure recipe comes from the folk medicine tradition. Mild rice milk is also a good source of folate, one of the vitamins that helps restore balance in the intestinal tract. Try the Rice Cure on its own or use it in place of commercial rice milk in any of the recipes in this book.

500 ml water
48 g rice
a drop or two of vanilla extract
1 teaspoon honey or to taste
dash cinnamon

Bring the water to boil in a saucepan. Add the rice, cover and simmer for twenty minutes. Add the vanilla extract and honey. Sprinkle with cinnamon. Strain and drink the liquid.

yield:
2 servings (250 ml each)

per serving with rice (included):
108 calories, 2 g protein, 24 g carbohydrates, 0.2 g fat, 0 mg cholesterol, 0.2 g dietary fibre, 7 mg sodium. A good source of folate.

cinnamon

In homeopathic, Asian, and folk medicine traditions, cinnamon is used to help stop diarrhoea. Cinnamon is also said to help bronchitis, colds, coughs, fever, indigestion, sore throat, and infection, and it may actually have the power to destroy bacteria. In a Kansas State University study, researchers found that when cinnamon was added to apple juice, the bacteria levels in the juice decreased.

Mildred's
Banana Rice Healer

My mother used to say that bananas, apples, tea, and chocolate could help overcome diarrhoea. I used banana and chocolate in this recipe, along with rice milk, which is easy on the digestive system. Bananas also supply potassium, an important mineral that can be depleted after a bout of diarrhoea. For an apple-carob rice healer, substitute carob rice milk for the chocolate rice milk and apple sauce for the banana.

> 250 ml chocolate-flavoured rice milk (or 250 ml plain rice
>   milk plus 2–3 teaspoons chocolate syrup)
> 1 medium banana
> dash salt
> 2 teaspoons honey or other sweetener (optional)

Combine the milk and banana in a blender and process until smooth. Stir in the salt. Add honey or sweetener if desired. Serve.

yield:
   1 serving (about 325 ml)

per serving:
   312 calories, 2 g protein, 73 g carbohydrates, 3 g fat, 0 mg cholesterol, 5 g dietary fibre, 250 mg sodium. High in vitamin B[6]; and vitamin C. A good source of vitamin E, potassium, and sodium.

Apple Ambush

The pectin in the carob and apple sauce in this drink helps stop diarrhoea. Carob also contains vegetable tannins, which help restore balance in the digestive tract. Don't forget that dash of salt; diarrhoea can deplete your body's sodium supply.

> 250 ml carob rice milk (or 250 ml rice milk plus 1 to
> 2 teaspoons carob powder)
> 125 ml unsweetened, natural apple sauce
> dash salt

Combine the carob rice milk and apple sauce and stir until smooth. Add the salt. Serve.

yield:
1 serving (375 ml)

per serving:
203 calories, 1 g protein, 46 g carbohydrates, 3 g fat, 0 mg cholesterol, 2 g dietary fibre, 242 mg sodium.

drink to your health

Vanilla Mellow

Mild rice milk is easy to digest, while yogurt with active cultures helps restore healthy bacteria in the intestines after diarrhoea or other digestive difficulties. Vanilla Mellow is high in carbohydrates, so it's calming, too. Try it before bedtime.

> 500 ml water
> 48 g white rice
> 2 tablespoons plain skimmed yogurt
> dash vanilla extract
> 1 teaspoon honey or other sweetener
> cinnamon (for garnish)

Bring the water to a boil. Add the rice, lower the heat to simmer, then cover and cook for 20 minutes. Strain the mixture, or leave it unstrained and eat the rice, too. Pour the liquid in a mug; stir in the yogurt, vanilla, and honey. Sprinkle with cinnamon and serve hot or cold.

yield:
2 servings (250 ml each)

per serving (with rice):
117 calories, 3 g protein, 26 g carbohydrates, 0.2 g fat, 0.3 mg cholesterol, 0.2 g dietary fibre, 19 mg sodium. A good source of folate.

Ultimate Egg Nog

This low-calorie version of the holiday favourite is a healthy beverage choice at any time of the year. It's high in protein and calcium, which help build strong bones and muscles. Egg substitutes are pasteurized, so they're safe to drink right out of the container. Fresh raw eggs should not be used because they can carry salmonella bacteria.

> 125 ml skimmed milk
> 1 teaspoon sugar
> ½ teaspoon vanilla extract
> 124 g egg substitute
> nutmeg (as garnish)

Combine the milk, sugar, vanilla extract, and egg substitute in a blender. Process just until foamy and well combined. Pour in a glass or mug, sprinkle with nutmeg, and serve cold.

yield:
> 1 serving (250 ml)

per serving:
> 125 calories, 16 g protein, 12 g carbohydrates, 0.2 g fat, 2 mg cholesterol, 0 g dietary fibre, 263 mg sodium. High in protein and calcium. A good source of vitamin A, riboflavin, vitamin D, iron, and potassium.

Mango Milk

Luscious mangoes are loaded with phytochemicals, antioxidants, and beta carotene, making this sweet milk drink nutritious as well as delicious. Because it contains magnesium and calcium, Mango Milk may also help prevent insomnia.

½ fresh mango
250 ml soya milk
1 teaspoon sunflower seeds

Combine the ingredients in a blender and purée.

yield:

1 serving (375 ml)

per serving:

214 calories, 11 g protein, 31 g carbohydrates, 6 g fat, 0 mg cholesterol, 2 g dietary fibre, 107 mg sodium. High in calcium, magnesium, protein, vitamin A, vitamin B¹², vitamin C, and vitamin E. A good source of vitamin B⁶, carbohydrates, folate, thiamine, vitamin D, pantothenic acid, iron, and potassium.

Blueberry Vision

During World War I, British flyers noticed that when they ate bilberry jam before flying at night, their night vision seemed to improve. Today experts know that bilberries and their cousins blueberries, cranberries, and blackberries, contain anthocyanosides, antioxidants that strengthen the capillaries in the retina. Anthocyanosides are also thought to be helpful in preventing age-related eye problems such as cataracts and macular degeneration.

250 ml vanilla-flavoured fortified soya milk
146 g fresh blueberries or 161 g frozen
dash cinnamon

Combine the soya milk and the blueberries in the blender and purée. Serve with a dash of cinnamon.

yield:
1 serving (325 ml)

per serving:
231 calories, 7 g protein, 43 g carbohydrates, 4 g fat, 0 mg cholesterol, 4 g dietary fibre, 99 mg sodium. High in vitamin A, vitamin B^{12}, vitamin C, vitamin E, and calcium. A good source of protein, carbohydrates, dietary fibre, thiamine, vitamin D, folate, magnesium, and potassium.

Meno-Magic

Temper the symptoms of menopause with this nutrient-dense drink. I also call this 'Quick Breakfast in a Glass' — it makes a healthy, well-balanced breakfast for those on the go.

> 250 ml chocolate-flavoured soya milk (or 250 ml plain
>   soya milk plus 1 or 2 teaspoons of chocolate syrup)
> 125 ml orange juice
> 1 tablespoon oat bran or wheat germ

Combine the ingredients in a large glass and whisk together.

yield:
    1 serving (375 ml)

per serving with oat bran:
    279 calories, 9 g protein, 52 g carbohydrates, 5 g fat, 0 cholesterol, 1 g dietary fibre, 40 mg isoflavones. High in vitamin C, vitamin D, folate, calcium, copper, and magnesium. A good source of protein, carbohydrates, iron, and potassium.

per serving with toasted wheat germ:
    291 calories, 10 g protein, 51 g carbohydrates, 6 g fat, 0 mg cholesterol, 1 g dietary fibre, 40 mg isoflavones. High in protein, vitamin C, vitamin D, folate, calcium, copper and magnesium. A good source of carbohydrates, iron, potassium, and zinc.

milks

soya and
isoflavones

Soya contains healthy isoflavones, daidzein and genistein, that may prevent heart disease and certain cancers. But when some soya foods (including soya hot dogs and soya burgers) are processed, isoflavones can be removed. Check food labels so you can be sure of a product's isoflavone content.

Studies indicate that soya protein will help lower cholesterol. To be effective, 30–50 mg per serving of isoflavones and 6.25 grams of soya protein are needed four times a day to lower cholesterol. A serving of soya that provides 30–50 mg isoflavones and 6.25 g soya protein are:

128 g cooked green soya beans
130 g cooked soya beans
64 g roasted soya butter
43 g roasted soya nuts
43 g soya flour
124 g firm tofu
250 ml soya milk
91 g cooked TVP (textured vegetable protein)
83 g tempeh

drink to your health

Strawberry Slider

Kids will love the Strawberry Slider's creamy pink colour and fruity taste, and it's so much more nutritious than the watered-down juice drinks that are popular today. It makes a great snack for adults, too: high in nutrients, low in fat and calories.

> 8 strawberries
> 2 tablespoons orange juice
> 150 ml vanilla-flavoured fortified soya milk or skimmed
> milk
> dash sugar (optional)

Combine the ingredients in a blender and process until smooth. Serve.

yield:
1 serving (250 ml)

per serving with vanilla-flavoured fortified soya milk:
142 calories, 5 g protein, 25 g carbohydrates, 2.4 g fat, 0 mg cholesterol, 2 g dietary fibre, 61 mg sodium. High in vitamin A, vitamin B^{12}, vitamin C, vitamin E, folate. A good source of protein, dietary fibre, thiamine, vitamin D, pantothenic acid, calcium, magnesium, and potassium.

Cucumber Cooler

Smooth, cool Cucumber Cooler, made with vegetables and low-fat dairy products, provides 249 milligrams of calcium – 25 per cent of the recommended Daily Value – for strong, healthy bones. Onion and garlic contribute phytochemicals to keep your immune system purring.

1 cucumber, peeled
125 ml skimmed or low-fat buttermilk
1 teaspoon chopped onion
1 clove garlic, minced
2 tablespoons plain non-fat yogurt
½ teaspoon chopped fresh chives

Cut peeled cucumber into chunks and place in a blender. Add the buttermilk, onion, garlic and yogurt and process. Pour into tall glass. Top with chopped chives. Serve.

yield:

1 serving (250 ml)

per serving:

106 calories, 8 g protein, 17 g carbohydrates, 2 g fat, 5 mg cholesterol, 2 g dietary fibre, 158 mg sodium. High in calcium, potassium, and a good source of protein, vitamin C, folate, and magnesium.

New Belly Bliss

A healthy belly is a blissful belly. The live cultures in this yogurt-based drink will help heal the digestive tract. Ginger, in addition to adding its distinctive flavour, will soothe your stomach and may help prevent ulcers.

125 ml non-fat plain yogurt
125 ml water
1/8 teaspoon grated fresh ginger

Combine the ingredients in a glass and whisk to combine. Serve.

yield:

1 serving (250 ml)

per serving:

69 calories, 7 g protein, 10 g carbohydrates, 0.2 g fat, 2 mg cholesterol, 0 g dietary fibre, 97 mg sodium. High in calcium. A good source of protein, riboflavin, and vitamin B[12].

The Peacemaker

When stress has got you down, turn to the Peacemaker. This creamy drink provides the key nutrients for stress relief: carbohydrates and vitamin B^6. And it's healthy in other ways, too. Bananas supply potassium, and prunes and raisins are packed with anti-ageing, immune-system-boosting antioxidants.

125 ml apple juice
125 ml red grape juice
4 pitted dried prunes
35 g raisins
2 whole cloves
2 whole allspice
½ banana
250 ml skimmed milk
125 ml plain non-fat yogurt

In a pot, combine juices, prunes, raisins, cloves and allspice. Bring to a boil. Lower heat and cook for 5 minutes. Remove from heat. Allow to set until cool. Remove the cloves and allspice. Add the banana and purée the mixture. Pour back into saucepan. Add the milk and yogurt and stir to combine. Serve warm or chilled.

yield:
2 servings (250 ml each)

per serving:

281 calories, 9 g protein, 60 g carbohydrates, 2 g fat, 6 mg cholesterol, 3 g dietary fibre, 118 mg sodium. High in carbohydrates, riboflavin, vitamin B^6, vitamin C, calcium, and potassium. A good source of protein, dietary fibre, vitamin A, thiamine, vitamin B^{12}, vitamin D, pantothenic acid, copper and magnesium.

milks

7

The recipes in this chapter are
those you'll use again and again
(and in other recipes in this book).
The concentrated sugar, mint, and
fruit syrups can be used to
sweeten any number of hot or
cold beverages, while super-
nutritious vegetable broth serves
as the perfect base for a variety of
soups. You'll find the other
'basics' included here to be
equally adaptable.

Watermelon Ice Cubes

Watermelon cubes make a wonderful addition to iced tea, soda water, and other drinks. As they melt, they add flavour and nutrition. Try making ice cubes using other fruits, too.

480 g cubed watermelon

Remove the seeds from the watermelon and purée in a blender or processor. Pour into ice cube trays and freeze. Store ice cubes in sealed plastic freezer bags and use as needed.

yield:
1 tray or 14–16 cubes

per cube:
10 calories, 0.2 g protein, 2 g carbohydrates, 0.1 g fat, 0 mg cholesterol, 0.2 g dietary fibre, 0.7 mg sodium.

migraine relief

For migraine headache relief, try sucking on a watermelon ice cube. Ice can prevent blood vessels from dilating painfully. The watermelon cubes provide a bit of sugar, which may also be helpful (low blood sugar can sometimes trigger migraines).

Cough Syrup

This recipe is a modified version of one I found in a collection of folk remedies called 'Mountain Makin's in the Smokies', published in 1957 by the Great Smoky Mountains Natural History Association. According to the book, Mrs Stanley Cooley learned to make cough syrup from her mother, who used it when her children had colds.

110 g flaxseed
375 ml water
76 g sugar
juice of 3 lemons
4 tablespoons honey

Add the flaxseed to a small saucepan filled with 375 ml water. Bring to a boil then lower heat to simmer. Cook until the liquid has boiled down to half its original amount. Remove from heat and stir in the sugar, lemon juice, and honey. Cool. Store in the refrigerator for up to one week or freeze. Give a spoonful as needed for coughs or sore throat.

yield:
250 ml

per tablespoon:
83 calories, 1 g protein, 15 g carbohydrates, 2 g fat, 0 mg cholesterol, 2 g dietary fibre, 4 mg sodium.

Sugar Syrup

Use this simple sugar syrup to sweeten iced beverages. It will blend with your drink instantly, without leaving a pile of undissolved sugar at the bottom of your glass.

> 125 ml water
> 153 g granulated sugar

Pour water into a saucepan and stir in sugar. Bring to a boil, stirring occasionally. To prevent a messy boil-over, keep your eye on the saucepan. As soon as you see the mixture boil, lower the heat to simmer. Simmer, stirring occasionally, for 5 minutes. Cool. Store in a jar in the refrigerator and use as needed.

yield:
250 ml

per teaspoon:
48 calories, 13 g carbohydrates, 0 g protein, 0 g fat, 0 mg cholesterol, 0 g dietary fibre, 0.4 mg sodium.

Ginger Syrup

This delicious syrup is used as a base for Homemade Ginger Ale (see page 132). You can also use a tablespoon or two to sweeten and flavour other drinks.

25 g chopped ginger (about 2 tablespoons)
250 ml water
1 tablespoon granulated sugar

In a small saucepan, combine the ginger, water, and sugar. Bring to a boil, then lower the heat and simmer, uncovered, for 10 minutes. Strain. Store in the refrigerator.

This recipe can be doubled or tripled depending on your needs.

yield:
250 ml

per tablespoon:
4 calories, 0 g protein, 1 g carbohydrates, 0 g fat, 0 mg cholesterol, 0 g dietary fibre, 1 mg sodium.

drink to your health

Ginger Juice and Hot Ginger Tea

Ginger juice adds the delicious snap of ginger to hot and cold teas and other beverages (try adding it to cranberry or pineapple juice). You can make fresh ginger juice by cutting a piece of ginger into thin slices, then pressing the slices through a garlic press. Or use a ginger grater that can be purchased in Asian supermarkets. Press grated ginger through a sieve to extract the juice.

Use ginger juice to make this relaxing tea, which will soothe the stomach and can help prevent motion sickness.

> 1 teaspoon grated or minced ginger root or 1 teaspoon
> ginger juice
> 250 ml boiling water

Combine the grated or minced ginger root or ginger juice with boiling water and steep for 5 minutes. Strain if necessary. Serve and sip.

yield:

1 serving (250 ml)

per serving:

1 calorie, 0 g protein, 0.3 g carbohydrates, 0 g fat, 0 mg cholesterol, 0 g dietary fibre, 7 mg sodium.

Mint Syrup

Homemade mint syrup adds sweetness and flavour to cold drinks or hot teas.

    250 ml water
    76 g granulated sugar
    10–12 fresh mint sprigs, chopped

Combine the water and sugar in a saucepan and bring to a boil. Simmer until the sugar is dissolved, about 5 minutes. Add the mint. Remove from heat and allow to cool. Strain. Store in a jar in the refrigerator and use as needed.

yield:
    250 ml

per tablespoon:
    24 calories, 6 g carbohydrates, 0 g fat, 0 g fibre, 0 mg cholesterol, 0 g dietary fibre, 0.5 mg sodium.

Sun Tea

Sun tea, simple to make and filled with healthy flavonoids, is clear and less bitter than tea made with boiling water. Try flavouring with added juices: mango, peach, orange, or lemon.

> 2.240 litres cold water
> 5 tea bags or 3–5 tablespoons loose green or black tea
> ice

Combine water and tea or tea bags in a glass container. Cover and place in the sun for 3 to 5 hours. Remove the bags or strain the tea; refrigerate. Serve cold with ice.

yield:

8 servings (250 ml each)

per serving:

2 calories, 0 g protein, 1 g carbohydrates, 0 g fat, 0 mg cholesterol, 0 g dietary fibre, 7 mg sodium.

Refrigerator Tea

You CAN make iced tea in the refrigerator, you'll just need to use more tea than usual — cold water does not draw flavour from the tea as well as hot water does.

> 1.120 litres cold water
> 5 tea bags or 3–5 tablespoons loose tea
> ice

Combine ingredients in a glass pitcher or jar. Cover. Refrigerate for 8 or more hours. Remove bags or strain. Serve over ice.

yield:
4 servings (250 ml each)

per serving:
0 calories, 0 g protein, 0 g carbohydrates, 0 g fat, 0 mg cholesterol, 0 g dietary fibre, 7 mg sodium.

drink to your health

fruit syrups

When you buy a fruit-flavoured soft drink, you're usually getting more sugar (in the form of high fructose corn syrup) than you bargained for. You can prepare fruit drinks at home and get more real fruit taste using these easy-to-make fruit syrups. For a light, delicious drink, mix 2 or 3 tablespoons of your favourite home-made syrup into a glass of water or soda water, add ice (and extra sweetener if necessary), and enjoy. Fruit syrups can also add flavour to any cold drink or hot beverage.

Blackberry Syrup

Only three ingredients are needed to make your own Blackberry Syrup from fresh or frozen blackberries. Use 2–3 tablespoons of this Blackberry Syrup in the Blackberry Sparkle recipe in the Cocktails and Other Sparkling Beverages section, or use it to add flavour and sweetness to your favourite beverage. Raspberries can be used in place of the blackberries.

> 306 g granulated sugar
> 250 ml water
> 324 g fresh blackberries or 340 g frozen unsweetened
>   blackberries

Stir the sugar and water together in a saucepan. Heat slowly to boiling, stirring occasionally. As soon as the mixture begins to boil, lower heat and simmer for 5 minutes. Add the berries, stir and simmer for another 10 minutes. Cool and strain. A thin, clear liquid will result. To remove more of the pulp from the berries, mash the berries through a sieve or cheesecloth lined strainer with a wooden spoon. Or a food mill can also be used to remove most of the seeds from the berries.

Store in a sealed jar in the refrigerator. Mix 2 or 3 tablespoons with plain soda water or water, or use to sweeten and flavour any drink.

yield:
550 ml

per 2 tablespoons:
98 calories, 0.2 g protein, 25 g carbohydrates, 0 g fat, 0 mg cholesterol, 1 g dietary fibre, 1 mg sodium.

drink to your health

Cranberry Syrup

This syrup does contain sugar, which helps temper the tartness of the berries. Use it in place of the blackberry syrup in the recipe for Blackberry Sparkle and you'll have a Cranberry Sparkle.

340 g granulated sugar
250 ml water
350 g fresh cranberries

Stir the sugar and water together in a saucepan. Heat slowly to boiling, stirring occasionally. As soon as the mixture begins to boil, lower heat and simmer for 5 minutes. Add rinsed cranberries and simmer another 10 minutes. Cool and strain using a food mill (some pulp and tiny seeds will remain) or press the berries, using a wooden spoon, through a cheesecloth lined strainer. If you would like a rich and clear red liquid, just allow the cranberry syrup to drip through a cheesecloth. Cool and refrigerate in a glass jar. Mix 2 or 3 tablespoons with plain soda water or water, or use to sweeten any drink.

yield:
550 ml

per 2 tablespoons:
95 calories, 0 g protein, 25 g carbohydrates, 0 g fat, 0 mg cholesterol, 0.8 g dietary fibre, 1 mg sodium.

Unsweetened Blueberry Syrup

Instead of adding the sugar to the blueberries immediately, this syrup is made without sugar and then a sugar of your choice can be added. Flavour soda water or your favourite beverage with 2–3 tablespoons of blueberry syrup and then add the sweetener of your choice to taste. Two to 3 teaspoons of granulated sugar, the sugar syrup in the Staples section, or ginger or mint syrup would work.

In a large glass, add 2–3 tablespoons of the blueberry syrup, 2–3 teaspoons of sugar, mint or ginger syrup, ¾ teaspoon of any non-caloric sweetener, fill the glass with water or soda water, stir and add ice.

> 250 ml water
> 328 g fresh blueberries or 340 g frozen unsweetened
> blueberries

Combine the blueberries and water in a saucepan. Bring to the boil and simmer for 10 minutes. Cool and press through a food mill, a cheese-cloth lined strainer, or a sieve. Store in a sealed jar in the refrigerator and use within a week or two.

yield:
375 ml

per 2 tablespoons:
15 calories, 0.1 g protein, 4 g carbohydrates, 0.2 g fat, 0 mg cholesterol, 1 g dietary fibre, 1 mg sodium.

drink to your health

Unsweetened Raspberry Syrup

Add unsweetened raspberry syrup and your favourite sweetener (caloric or non-caloric) to soda water or the beverage of your choice. Delicious!

> 250 ml water
> 184 g fresh raspberries or 340 g frozen unsweetened
>   raspberries
> 6 teaspoons non-caloric sweetener

Wash the fresh raspberries if using those. Add the raspberries and the water to a saucepan. Bring the mixture to a boil, lower the heat and simmer for 10 minutes. Cool slightly. Press through a sieve or food mill. You will have about 300 ml. To this stir in 2 teaspoons of non-caloric sweetener of your choice. Store in a sealed jar in the refrigerator and use within a week or two.

yield:
> 300 ml

per 2 tablespoons:
> 17 calories, 0.3 g protein, 4 g carbohydrates, 0.2 g fat, 0 mg cholesterol, 1 mg sodium.

Vegetable Broth

Use this low-sodium vegetable broth as a base in soup recipes. It's also delicious enough to enjoy plain or with cooked rice, millet, barley or other grains for added fibre.

Shiitake mushrooms make this broth a nutritional knock-out. They're high in B vitamins and contain immune system strengthening phytochemicals and cholesterol-lowering eritadenine. If you can't find fresh shiitake, substitute maiitake, enoki, or oyster mushrooms. White button mushrooms can also be used; they'll provide good flavour and B vitamins but contain few phytochemicals.

2 teaspoons olive oil
270 g chopped shallots or onions
3 garlic cloves, minced
242 g chopped celery
274 g chopped carrots
100 g fresh shiitake mushrooms, chopped
15 g chopped fresh parsley
2 bay leaves
1 teaspoon dried thyme
3360 ml water

Heat the olive oil in a soup pot. Add the shallots or onions, garlic, celery, carrots, and mushrooms. Sauté for several minutes until the onions are softened. Add the parsley, bay leaves, thyme, and water. Bring to a boil, then lower the heat to a simmer. Cover and cook for 1½ hours. Cool and strain. Use immediately or freeze in 250 ml or 500 ml quantities for use in future recipes.

drink to your health

yield:

8 servings (2.240 litres)

per cup:

79 calories, 2 g protein, 11 g carbohydrates, 4 g fat, 0 mg cholesterol, 0 g dietary fibre, 52 mg sodium. High in vitamin A. A good source of vitamin B^6 and folate.

Who knew improving your vitality and immunity could be this delicious? Whether you want to slow down the effects of ageing, relieve arthritis or a headache, lower your cholesterol levels, help to prevent heart disease or overcome insomnia, or get over a cold or the flu, you can drink to your health. Use the ailments index to identify those drinks that are best-suited to help you address your particular condition.

ailments index

anti-ageing

To lengthen your life, help fight the effects of ageing, and prevent age-related diseases like cancer and heart disease, choose foods that are high in antioxidants: vitamins C and E, selenium, carotenoids (including beta carotene), monounsaturated fats, and healing phytochemicals. Blueberries and cranberries are particularly noted for their anti-ageing properties.

recommended for fighting the effects of ageing:

Mike's Blueberry Egg Cream

Mango Sunrise

Ginger Mango Supersmoothie

Orange Julia

Soya Peach Blueberry Perk-Up

Tomato Veggie Powerhouse

appetite loss/ low body weight

To gain weight, you need to increase your caloric intake. But not just any calories will do. To ensure healthy weight gain, eat foods that provide calories and nutrition. If you're too busy to stop for a full meal, drink a nutrient-dense beverage on the run.

Brewer's yeast, an excellent source of B vitamins, can act as an appetite stimulant, as can the following herbs: caraway, cardamom, chamomile, chicory, cinnamon, coriander, dill, fenugreek, ginger, lemon balm, peppermint, rosemary, sage, and turmeric.

recommended for healthy weight gain:

Purple Protein Power Shake

Lemon Balm Anxiety Reducer

Nutrient-Dense Pear-Avocado Abundance

Ginger Apricot Support

Morning Superstart

Soya Peach Blueberry Perk-Up

arteriosclerosis

To prevent arteriosclerosis, or hardening of the arteries, keep your cholesterol level low and choose foods that are low in fat and high in soluble fibre. Keep intake of saturated fats (animal and dairy fats such as meat, milk and cheese) and trans- or hydrogenated fats (vegetable shortening and margarine) to a minimum.

Certain nutrients, including the antioxidants, can also help lower cholesterol levels. The plant chemicals such as quercetin, which is found in apples, onions, and black tea, can lower cholesterol, and resveratrol, found in red wine or red grapes, may also be helpful. Garlic has blood-thinning properties. To help lower homocysteine levels, which causes blood vessel damage, increase the folate in your diet.

recommended for the prevention of arteriosclerosis:

Orange Ginger Quencher
Sun Tea and Refrigerator Tea
Grape Tea
Papaya Zinger
High-C
Ginger Apricot Support
Apple Parsnip Power
Blackberry Wine Cooler

anaemia

General weakness, loss of appetite, dizziness, inability to concentrate, headache, and apathy can be signs of iron-deficiency anaemia, or lack of iron in the blood. Most common in pregnant women and persons with chronic illnesses, iron-deficiency anaemia can be detected with a simple blood test performed by your doctor.

To prevent or reverse iron-deficiency anaemia, eat foods that are rich in iron (leafy green vegetables, fish, and blackstrap molasses) and the B vitamins.

arthritis

Because rheumatoid arthritis is an autoimmune disease, foods that strengthen the immune system – fruits, vegetables, whole grains – can help patients with the condition. Antioxidants can strengthen the immune system and help slow joint deterioration. Choose foods that are rich in beta carotene (spinach and other dark leafy vegetables, apricots and other yellow or deep orange vegetables) and vitamin C (especially cantaloupe melon, broccoli, strawberries, peppers and cranberry juice). In the folk medicine tradition, cherries are a remedy for arthritis.

High-fat diets can make arthritis worse, so avoid saturated fats such as those found in meats and dairy products. Some patients may notice that their pain or arthritis discomfort increases when they eat certain foods, particularly wheat products, dairy products, corn, citrus, and eggs. Talk to your doctor, and keep a food diary to see how certain foods affect your body. Try eliminating vegetables in the nightshade family – tomatoes, white potatoes, peppers, and aubergines – from your diet.

Some people believe that wearing a copper bracelet offers arthritis relief, so eating foods that are rich in copper (whole grains, leafy green vegetables, almonds and other nuts) might be beneficial. Ginger and turmeric, herbs with anti-inflammatory properties, may also help.

Blackberry Sparkle
Creamy Split Pea Soup
Melon Mango Invigorator
Oyster Stew
Hot Ginger Tea
Green Ginger Tea

athletic injuries

Maintain a healthy, well-balanced diet when your body is healing from an athletic injury. Complex carbohydrates will help maintain muscle strength, while vitamin E can help prevent muscle soreness. And magnesium will keep muscles flexible so that injury can be avoided. Drink plenty of water to help prevent muscle spasms and cramps.

To help heal broken or fractured bones, eat a diet rich in the B vitamins, zinc, calcium, vitamin D, and protein.

recommended for those with athletic injuries:
One-Two Punch
Caribbean Powerhouse
Melon Mango Invigorator
Morning Superstart
Purple Protein Power Shake
Hi-Pro

bladder or
urinary tract infections

Bacterial infections in the bladder or urethra are particularly common in women. If you have a bladder or urinary tract infection, try drinking a glass of water every hour for eight hours to dilute the urine and help flush out bacteria. Cranberry and blueberry juice can also help eliminate unwanted bacteria from the bladder and urinary tract.

recommended for prevention and relief of bladder or urinary tract infections:

UTI Cocktail

Good Time Party Punch

Unsweetened Blueberry Syrup

Cranberry Fizz

Tummy Rescue Remedy

Mike's Blueberry Egg Cream

cancer

Experts believe that diet can play a crucial role in reducing the risk of cancer, particularly cancer of the breast, bowel, and prostate. Eating the recommended five servings of fruits and vegetables each day may reduce the rate of some cancers by more than 20 per cent.

In October 1998, the American Institute for Cancer Research released their International Report on Cancer Prevention. Among their recommendations for cancer prevention:

- Eat a plant-based diet, one that is rich in a variety of vegetables, fruits, legumes, and minimally processed foods.
- Maintain a healthy weight. Limit weight gain during adulthood to less than 11 pounds.
- Eat five or more servings a day of a variety of fruits and vegetables.
- Eat seven or more servings a day of a variety of grains, legumes, and root vegetables.
- Limit consumption of refined sugar.
- Avoid alcoholic beverages, or limit yourself to no more than two each day (no more than one a day for women).
- Limit fatty and salty foods. Choose modest amounts of appropriate vegetable oils.
- Avoid eating charred foods. Consume grilled or steamed meat and fish or cured and smoked meats only occasionally.

recommended for cancer prevention:
Cancer Phyter
High-C
Melon Mango Invigorator
Mango Milk with Green Tea
Orange Froth
Creamy Split Pea Soup
My Best Gazpacho
Phyto-Favourite
Hot Garlic, Carrot and Broccoli Soup

cholesterol

Heart disease, the leading cause of illness and death in the western world, is related to high blood pressure and high blood cholesterol. A cholesterol level of 200 or lower is recommended.

A healthy diet that is low in cholesterol, fat, trans- and saturated fat will help reduce blood cholesterol. Eat plenty of fruits, vegetables, and whole grains. Soluble fibre – found in oats, rice, barley, and dried beans – can also help lower blood cholesterol levels.

recommended for lowering cholesterol:
Mug o' Barley
Mildred's Banana Rice Healer
Sy's Lime Rickey
Raspberry Rumble

chronic fatigue syndrome

Foods that are high in protein, fibre, vitamins, and magnesium can help the fatigue associated with Chronic Fatigue Syndrome. Try a high-fibre, high-protein drink in the morning or as a snack for an energy boost.

Allergies and food sensitivities can also contribute to Chronic Fatigue Syndrome. While allergies usually last a lifetime, food sensitivities can change with time and are usually associated with food groups, such as citrus fruits or milk products. Try changing the foods you eat and see how you feel. The most common food allergies involve corn, eggs, milk, sugar, and wheat.

Some experts believe Chronic Fatigue Syndrome may be related to a low blood pressure syndrome called Neurally Mediated Hypotension. A moderate salt intake and higher liquid consumption can be helpful for persons with Neurally Mediated Hypotension and may therefore benefit those with Chronic Fatigue Syndrome as well.

recommended for those with chronic fatigue syndrome:
Soya Peach Blueberry Perk-Up
Soya Peach Strawberry Smoothie
Avocado Smoothie
Hi-Pro
Tomato Veggie Powerhouse
Creamy Split Pea Soup

colds and bronchitis

A cure for the common cold has eluded scientists for decades. But research is continuing to prove that herbs and nutrients can help prevent and shorten the duration of colds and respiratory infections like bronchitis. Hot drinks are also comforting for cold sufferers; they help get the mucous flowing and raise the body temperature, stimulating the immune system to increase its production of infection fighting antibodies.

To prevent a cold or to help heal one, try increasing your intake of one or more of the nutrients listed here:

Vitamin C, abundant in tropical and citrus fruits, boosts the immune system to help fight off infections.

drinks high in vitamin C include:
Good Time Party Punch
High C

Elizabeth's Healing Cocktail
Lemon Aid
Raspberry Lemon Aid
Leanne's Orange Passion

Echinacea, long used by Native Americans to treat a variety of conditions, seems to support the immune system by increasing the production and activity of white blood cells. Try taking echinacea when you have a cold or a sore throat. If used for longer than 6 to 8 weeks for cold prevention, echinacea's beneficial effects can diminish.

Talk to your doctor before using echinacea if you have lupus, tuberculosis, or multiple sclerosis, or if you are allergic to flowers in the daisy family. And don't take echinacea if you're taking corticosteroids (like Decadron, prednisone) or Cyclosporine (Neoral, Sandimmune).

drinks containing echinacea include:
Echinacea Tea with Lemon and Honey
Aromatic Astragalus Tea

Zinc strengthens the immune system and may help shorten the duration of a cold.

drinks high in zinc include:
Tomato Veggie Powerhouse
Jewish Penicillin Chicken Stock
Creamy Split Pea Soup
Oyster Stew

Cayenne and other hot peppers act as expectorants and decongestants.

drinks that contain cayenne and other hot peppers include:
Hot Garlic, Carrot and Broccoli Soup
Jewish Penicillin

drink to your health

Hot beverages act as decongestants and soothers.

hot beverages include:
Phyto-Favourite
Creamy Shiitake Broth
Licorice Root Soother
Hot Garlic, Carrot and Broccoli Soup
Doubly Green Tea
Jewish Penicillin

cold sores

Foods high in lysine, such as corn, kidney beans, and split peas, can help relieve and prevent cold sores, which are caused by the Herpes Simplex virus. Avoid citrus and other acid foods, which can be painful and irritating, and avoid nuts, chocolate, and seeds. These latter contain the amino acid that is food for the virus. Smooth cream soups and milkshakes can be soothing.

recommended for soothing cold sores:
Creamy Split Pea Soup
New-Fashioned Vanilla Milkshake

constipation

To keep bowel movements regular and prevent constipation, drink plenty of water (six to eight glasses a day) and make sure you're eating enough fibre. Twenty-five to thirty-five grams of dietary fibre per day are recommended. If you're not used to eating that much fibre, increase your daily intake slowly. High fibre foods include vegetables, especially peas, beans, and broccoli; bran cereals and wheat bran; oat bran; whole grains; and fruits, particularly dried fruits such as raisins, figs, and prunes. You can also add fibre to your diet using a fibre supplement such as psyllium or powdered flaxseed.

Other foods and beverages that can help relieve constipation include coffee, perhaps because the caffeine stimulates the digestive system; prunes and prune juice, which contain a bowel stimulant called dihydroxyphenyl isatin; and grapes and raisins, which contain tartaric acid, a natural laxative.

Note: See your doctor if your constipation is accompanied by pain, fever, or blood.

recommended for the relief of constipation:
Tutti Fruiti on the Rocks
Faux Café
Psyllium Soother
Prune-Raisin Smoothie
Creamy Split Pea Soup

diarrhoea

Diarrhoea can be caused by certain foods or by an infection, virus, or food poisoning. Whatever the cause, when you have diarrhoea you'll need to replace lost fluids by drinking lots of water, herb and black or green teas, mineral water, flat cola beverages, diluted sports drinks, or flat ginger ale. Avoid carbonated beverages, which can cause gas and add to the discomfort. Start eating solid foods and fibre gradually as your condition improves. Pectin, found in apples and bananas, can help firm the stools. (Try apple sauce rather than apple juice, which can contribute to diarrhoea.)

Because it involves fluid loss, diarrhoea can also drain your body of vital electrolytes. Replace lost sodium by drinking bouillon, diluted sports drinks, and soya, rice, or barley miso. Bananas will help firm stools and replace lost potassium.

Folate and berry leaf teas (blackberry, blueberry, and raspberry) can help heal and soothe an irritated colon. Yogurt with live cultures helps replace good bacteria in the intestines.

The tannins in green tea also combat diarrhoea; the longer the tea is

drink to your health

steeped, the more tannins the tea will contain. The problem, however, is that green tea also contains caffeine, which can exacerbate a diarrhoea problem. Try drinking decaffeinated green tea. Or, because most of the caffeine from tea is drawn into the water in the first minute of steeping, steep green tea for one minute, pour the liquid away, then use the bag again to get more tannins and less caffeine. Use discretion and moderation, and see what works best for you.

If diarrhoea lasts more than a few days, see a doctor.

recommended for treatment of diarrhoea:

The Rice Cure

Mildred's Banana Rice Healer

Apple Ambush

Greenberry Tea

Souper Miso

Vanilla Mellow

diverticulosis

Diverticula, or pouches, form in the intestines as we age. Diverticulosis is the painful condition that occurs when these pouches become inflamed and infected.

To prevent diverticulosis, eat a low-fat, high-fibre diet (20 to 25 grams of fibre daily), drink at least 8 glasses of water a day, and lower your stress level. Avoid low-fibre, processed foods such as white bread, white rice, crackers and biscuits, and try to include some wheat bran in your diet. Like psyllium and flaxseed, wheat bran absorbs water in our bodies, softening the stools and adding bulk so that they can move smoothly through the intestines.

Once you have diverticulosis and the intestinal pouches are infected, however, a high-fibre diet can make the problem worse. Until the infection is over, most types of fibre should be avoided. Do not eat popcorn, celery, nuts, seeds, or seeded foods like tomatoes, cucumbers, and raspberries. So that you are not constipated during the healing process, apples, peaches, bananas, pears, oranges, seedless grapes, raisins, prunes, carrots, lettuce, bran and bran cereals, and whole wheat breads may be eaten in moderation.

recommended for the prevention of diverticulosis:
  Mug o' Barley
  Watermelon Chamomile Frosty
  Creamy Split Pea Soup
  Psyllium Soother
  Blueberry Smoothie
  Pear and Blueberry Smoothie

fibromyalgia

Fibromyalgia, often called the 'baby boomers' disease,' is an immune system disorder characterized by fatigue and pain in the muscles and connective tissues. At this time there is no cure for fibromyalgia but medication, exercise, and lifestyle changes have allowed patients to manage their symptoms and improve their quality of life.

Doctors recommend that patients with fibromyalgia eat a healthy diet that is low in caffeine, sugar, and fat, and high in fibre. And magnesium and malic acid have been shown to alleviate some of the symptoms. High-magnesium foods include soya and soya products, rice, bananas, dark leafy greens, avocado, blackstrap molasses, oysters, and yogurt. Malic acid is found naturally in apples and can be taken as a dietary supplement. It's also used commercially to control pH levels in processed foods; when used, it will appear on a product's list of ingredients.

recommended for those with fibromyalgia:
  Nutrient-Dense Pear-Avocado Abundance
  Golden Quencher
  Avocado Smoothie
  Vanilla Mellow
  Spirit Lifting St John's Wort Tea
  Pumpkin Apple Healer

drink to your health

hangover

To help relieve the pain and discomfort of a hangover, and to prevent the dehydration associated with alcohol consumption, drink plenty of liquids, especially water and those containing fructose. Found naturally in honey, tomato juice, and any fruit juice, fructose is quickly absorbed into the bloodstream. It will raise your energy level and can help your body burn off alcohol. (Some experts also believe that vitamin C can help clear the body of alcohol.) Caffeine and cold drinks can help shrink blood vessels in the brain and relieve alcohol-related headaches.

recommended for hangover relief:
Iced Mochaccino

Sy's Lime Rickey

Quick Comeback

Kiwi Strawberry Smoothie

headache

Stress and tension headaches are caused by tightness in the head and neck muscles. For drinks that may help relieve stress or tension headaches, see Stress.

Vascular or migraine type headaches are caused when the blood vessels in the brain dilate. Vascular headaches can be triggered by hormones, hunger, changes in altitude, changes in weather, bright or flashing lights, smoking, or food allergy.

If you suffer from migraines, avoid foods that may trigger them, including chocolate, red wine, aged cheeses, monosodium glutamate (MSG), and hot dogs. These foods contain tyramine, an amino acid that causes the blood vessels first to constrict and then to dilate, causing headache pain. Caffeine, ice water, and cold drinks can bring headache relief by helping enlarged arteries contract.

Among the nutrients believed to help prevent migraine headaches are magnesium (found in bran, wheat germ, soya, peanut butter, and yogurt); calcium and vitamin D (found in milk and enriched soya milk); and riboflavin (found in dairy foods, eggs, leafy vegetables and enriched and whole grains).

Ginger may also help prevent migraines by blocking the action of the prostaglandins that cause pain and inflammation in blood vessels. Add $1/3$ teaspoon of powdered ginger to your favourite beverage when you feel a migraine coming on.

recommended for migraine relief:
 Hot Ginger Tea
 Iced Mochaccino
 Refrigerator and Sun Tea
 Soothing Spearmint Tea
 Watermelon Ice Cubes
 Tummy Rescue Remedy

age-related hearing loss

Recent studies have shown that age-related hearing loss may be related to low levels of vitamin B^{12} and folate in the bloodstream. Try increasing the amount of these nutrients in your daily diet.

recommended for the prevention of age-related hearing loss:
 Avocado Smoothie
 Ginger Mango Supersmoothie
 Morning Superstart

heart disease

One of the leading causes of illness and death, heart disease is related to and can be caused by high blood pressure and high cholesterol. To protect yourself against heart disease, maintain a diet that is high in fruits, vegetables, and low-fat dairy foods, and low in sodium, saturated fat, and total fat. Oat bran and dried beans are high in soluble fibre and can help lower cholesterol levels and the risk of heart disease. The minerals potassium, magnesium, and calcium, which are often lacking in the Western diet, are important in preventing high blood pressure and heart disease.

The flavonoids in red wine, green tea, and fruits and vegetables, the calcium in skimmed milk, the mono fat in almonds, and the omega-3 fatty acids in fish and flax can also help prevent heart disease.

(Other major factors for developing heart disease include stress, smoking, lack of exercise, and obesity. To protect your heart health, get plenty of exercise, use stress reduction techniques, maintain a normal body weight, and avoid tobacco products.)

recommended for the prevention of heart disease:

Ginger Apricot Support

Melon Mango Invigorator

Soya Peach Blueberry Perk-Up

Manhattan Clam Chowder

Oyster Stew

Strawberry Wine Cooler

Blackberry Wine Cooler

Good Time Party Punch

Kiwi Soya Smoothie

Mighty Blue Healer

haemorrhoids

Fibre! The best way to prevent the pain and itching of haemorrhoids is to eat at least 25 grams of fibre every day. Foods that are high in fibre are vegetables, fruits, nuts and whole grains. Psyllium, flaxseed, bran, and wheat germ add fibre to the diet and bulk to the stool. Avoid coffee and caffeine drinks, which have diuretic properties that can contribute to hard stools.

Folate, potassium, selenium, zinc, vitamin A, vitamin C, vitamin E, and protein are recommended as healing nutrients for haemorrhoids.

recommended for the prevention of haemorrhoids:
Mighty Blue Healer
Creamy Split Pea Soup
Prune-Raisin Smoothie
Soothing Spearmint Tea

high blood pressure

A diet rich in fruits, vegetables and low-fat dairy foods and low in saturated fat, total fat, and sodium is recommended for persons with high blood pressure.

Garlic and onion are said to reduce high blood pressure; red wine can help lower blood pressure when used in moderation.

Minerals that may help lower or control blood pressure include calcium (found in low-fat yogurt or milk, buttermilk, and fortified soya milks) potassium, and magnesium.

**recommended to prevent or control
high blood pressure:**
Blackberry Wine Cooler
Nutrient-Dense Pear-Avocado Abundance
Grape Tea
Green Tea with Punch
Blueberry Smoothie
High Po

hypoglycaemia

Low blood sugar can cause weakness, hunger, nervousness, dizziness, trembling, or perspiration. Small, frequent meals that include whole grains, beans, soya products, and foods that are high in protein, complex carbohydrates, and fibre can help keep blood sugar levels even. Persons with hypoglycaemia should avoid caffeine and alcohol.

Chromium, a mineral found in whole grains, brewer's yeast,

molasses, eggs and cheese, helps convert glucose into energy, and may also help keep blood sugar levels even.

recommended for those with hypoglycaemia:
Ultimate Egg Nog
Homemade Beetroot Borscht
Savoury Almond Vegetable Soup
Creamy Split Pea Soup
Soya Peach Blueberry Perk-Up

insomnia

Insomnia can be caused by stress, hunger, menopausal or post menopausal hormone shifts, or carbohydrate needs. The night can also loom long due to pain, too much caffeine, daytime naps, or inadequate exercise.

Hot, herbal, caffeine-free teas sipped slowly before bedtime can be helpful in inducing sleep and relaxation. Passion flower, lemon balm, chamomile, linden flower, skullcap, valerian, and lavender, are known for their calming effects.

recommended for treatment of insomnia:
Passion Flower Bedtime Tea
Grandmother Rose's Cup of Tea
My Best Gazpacho
Mango Milk
Lemon Balm Anxiety Reducer
Soothing Spearmint Tea
Calming Almond Milk

intestinal virus
(gastroenteritis or stomach flu)

Flat ginger ale, Mom's old stand-by for stomach flu, can actually help when a person has an intestinal virus; ginger helps calm an upset stomach and relieves digestive problems. Ginger or stomach-soothing mint teas can also be slowly sipped to help calm the stomach and replace lost liquids.

Fluid replacement is important when flu is accompanied by vomiting. Persons who are vomiting should sip water, tea, or mineral water until they are able to try bland, solid foods, such as mashed potatoes and rice.

If flu symptoms last more than two to three days, call your doctor.

recommended for treatment of an intestinal virus or flu:
Hot Ginger Tea
Tummy Rescue Remedy

irritable bowel syndrome

Irritable Bowel Syndrome (IBS) can involve diarrhoea, constipation, flatulence, or alternating diarrhoea and constipation. While stress is considered a major factor in the condition, depression, caffeine, laxatives, gastrointestinal illness, antibiotics, and sleep irregularity can also contribute.

A healthy diet that is low in fat and contains moderate amounts of fibre can help calm irritable bowels. (Fibre helps keep the stools soft and easy to pass, but too much fibre can cause wind and bloating.) Drink at least eight glasses of water a day to help ensure regularity.

Hot, caffeine-free teas (try chamomile or lemon balm) may help sufferers of Irritable Bowel Syndrome because they are soothing.

recommended for those with irritable bowel syndrome:
Soothing Spearmint Tea
Lemon Balm Anxiety Reducer
Mint Syrup
Chocolate Kiwi Surprise
Psyllium Soother
Licorice Root Soother

drink to your health

macular degeneration

Macular degeneration, which generally occurs in persons over the age of 55, is a genetic disease that affects the retina and can lead to blindness. There is no cure for the disease once it occurs, but research suggests that zinc may help protect the eye from macular damage. Zinc-rich foods include oysters, clams, shrimp, beef and beef stock, chicken and chicken stock, yogurt, wheat germ, soya, peanut butter, and miso.

recommended to prevent macular degeneration:

    Oyster Stew
    Jewish Penicillin
    Blueberry Smoothie
    Pear and Blueberry Smoothie

menopausal symptoms

Exercise and the right diet may help reduce the symptoms of menopause, which include hot flushes, insomnia, forgetfulness, loss of creativity, osteoporosis, vaginal dryness, and lessened sexual desire. The right diet should include healthy, low-fat foods and foods that contain vitamin E and fish oils.

Foods that are high in phytoestrogens replace lost oestrogen naturally and can also help relieve symptoms. Try including whole wheat, flax, broccoli, cauliflower, split peas, spinach, coffee, apples, barley, carrots, cherries, chick peas, garlic, yams, and soya in your diet. Some researchers believe that just two servings of soya a day can bring results. A serving of soya would be 250 ml of soya milk, 87 g of soya beans, 57 g of roasted soya nuts, 28 g of soya flour, 46 g of textured vegetable protein (TVP), or 125 g of tofu. The herbs oregano, thyme, and turmeric may also have some oestrogenic properties.

After menopause, the metabolism slows and fewer calories are needed to maintain a healthy weight, so lower calorie and nutrient-dense foods are recommended. Because hormonal changes can increase the risk for heart disease, an increase in the antioxidant vitamins would also be beneficial. And because osteoporosis is more common after menopause, extra calcium should be included in the diet. (See Osteoporosis.)

recommended for the relief of menopausal symptoms:
Meno-Magic
Savoury Almond Vegetable Soup
Soya Do It
Hot Garlic, Carrot and Broccoli Soup

mood elevating/depression

Research suggests that a high-carbohydrate, low-protein diet can improve mood. High carbohydrate foods supply the body with tryptophan, which increases the level of the feel-good neurotransmitter serotonin in the brain.

Eating chocolate, cayenne peppers, and other hot peppers, may help, too: these foods stimulate the production of endorphins, natural tranquillizers that make a person feel calm and increase positive feelings of well-being.

S-adenosyl-L-methionine, better known as SAMe, is another substance that may affect mood-controlling neurotransmitters in the brain. SAMe is created from methionine, an amino acid or protein found in soya, beans, and meat. SAMe is now being sold as an antidepressant or supplement. However, if your body is lacking in vitamin B^{12}, vitamin B^6 or folate, the methionine in SAMe will convert to homocysteine, which is bad for the heart. If you're taking SAMe, make sure you're eating plenty of whole grains, beans, fish, poultry, and leafy green vegetables.

The herb St John's Wort is also thought to enhance serotonin levels and relieve feelings of depression.

recommended for mood elevation:
Chocolate Kiwi Surprise
Spirit Lifting St John's Wort Tea

New-Fashioned Vanilla Milkshake
Purple Protein Power Shake
Cocoa Fruit Smoothie

motion sickness

Ginger, which calms the stomach, can be used to prevent and alleviate
motion sickness.

recommended for the prevention
and treatment of motion sickness:
Ginger Syrup
Homemade Ginger Ale

osteoporosis

To prevent osteoporosis, include calcium-rich dairy products and leafy
green vegetables in your diet, especially if you are female and post-
menopausal. Avoid caffeine, alcohol, and foods that are high in
phosphorus, including red meat and soft drinks. Foods that are high
in phytoestrogens, particularly foods containing soya, can also promote
bone strength.

Your body needs vitamin D to absorb calcium from the foods you
eat. Foods that are rich in vitamin D include tuna, salmon, and enriched
milk products. You can also get vitamin D by spending a little time in
the sun – just 10 to 30 minutes a week will do the trick.

recommended for the prevention of osteoporosis:
Cucumber Cooler
Strawberry Slider
Caribbean Powerhouse
Soya Do It
Calming Almond Milk

premenstrual syndrome

To reduce the symptoms of premenstrual syndrome (PMS), which include bloating, mood changes and depression, acne, headaches, fatigue, weight gain, breast tenderness, and cravings for sugary or salty foods, stick to a low-fat, high-fibre diet. Avoid foods that are high in sugar, caffeine, and sodium (which contributes to bloating).

Foods that are high in complex carbohydrates may give some relief from mood swings. Vitamin B^6 (a natural diuretic that can relieve bloating), vitamin E (to relieve breast tenderness), vitamin A, and the minerals magnesium and calcium are recommended.

recommended for the prevention or relief of PMS symptoms:

Cocoa Fruit Smoothie

Mellow Mama

Hot Garlic, Carrot and Broccoli Soup

Mango Milk

stomach ulcers

Abdominal pain between meals or after drinking alcohol or acidic beverages such as orange juice, coffee, tea, or colas, can signal the presence of an ulcer. If you think you have an ulcer, see your doctor, who can diagnose the source of your pain and will prescribe antibiotics if necessary (ulcers are believed to be caused by bacterial infections).

A healthy diet that is low in fat and high in fibre can help prevent ulcers. And stress does play a role: even though ulcers are caused by bacterial infections, you are more likely to develop an ulcer if you are under stress.

If you are taking antibiotics for your ulcer, your medication may be killing off 'friendly' bacteria along with the harmful bacteria in your body. Yogurt with lives cultures may help to restore the beneficial bacteria that antibiotics can eliminate.

drink to your health

recommended for the prevention of stomach ulcers:

Elizabeth's Healing Cocktail
New Belly Bliss
Island Powerhouse
Vanilla Mellow
The Rice Cure
The Peacemaker

stress

A stress-fighting diet is centred around fruits, vegetables and whole grains. Avoid high-fat foods and limit your caffeine intake. Learn to relax with a hot cup of herbal tea in the middle of the day – chamomile and lemon balm are soothing and relaxing.

recommended for stress reduction:

The Peacemaker
Kiwi Strawberry Smoothie
Lemon Balm Anxiety Reducer
Ginger Yogurt Support
Soothing Spearmint Tea

varicose veins

The best way to prevent varicose veins is to keep your circulation system in tip-top shape. Drink plenty of fluids, at least 8 glasses of water each day, to promote circulation. High-vitamin and -mineral foods – vegetables, fruits, and whole grains – are excellent for keeping veins in good condition, as are antioxidants, especially vitamins C and E.

Bioflavonoids, found in citrus fruits, apricots, blueberries, black-berries, apples, onions, cherries, and green tea, help maintain vascular strength. They protect the blood vessels and reduce platelet aggregation, acting as natural blood thinners.

recommended for the prevention of varicose veins:

Fresh Mint Tinkle

Grape Tea

Apple Parsnip Power

Pear and Blueberry Smoothie

Morning Superstart

Frosty Apricot Mint Cooler

wind and wind pains

Wind is a natural byproduct of digestion. Some foods, however, produce more wind when they are digested than others do. Beans are infamous for their wind-producing properties – their high carbohydrate content results in extra wind when digested. (Soya beans are higher in protein and are easier to digest.) Milk products can cause painful wind, especially in those that are lactose-intolerant. If milk is a problem for you, try low-lactose or lactose-free varieties, acidophilus milk, rice milk, soya milk, or nut milks.

Wind is also caused when there is excess air in the stomach, which can result from eating too fast, eating foods that are beaten (such as blender drinks), drinking carbonated drinks, drinking through a straw, riding a bike with your mouth open, or chewing gum.

For relief and to aid in digestion, peppermint and chamomile are recommended. Anise, caraway, coriander, ginger, and turmeric can also be helpful.

recommended to relieve wind and to aid in digestion:

Basil Tea

Soothing Spearmint Tea

Lemon Balm Anxiety Reducer

Resources

Teas

Your local health food shop, supermarket and delicatessen will carry a range of traditional, herbal and non-herbal teas, but you might like to check out the following web sites which offer interesting background information on the subject of tea and on-line ordering and delivery services:

Grey's Teas: With over 50 loose teas to choose from, some quite hard to find, this on-line company offers a reliable and free delivery service to UK customers. They also sell reusable tea infusers. *www.greysteas.co.uk*

Twinings Herbal Teas: The Internet Health Library offers web site news and information on a number of health-related issues. Click on the *herbal tea* listing to find out about Twinings Teas and Herbal Infusions, and how to order them. *www.internethealthlibrary.com*

Yogi brand Echinacea Tea: A good flavoured tea which contains many ingredients, including astragalus root, fennel, cardamom, clove, black pepper, and mint. *www.yogitea.com*

Seelect Tea: This range of teas has been specially formulated to enhance wellbeing. Try their Balance and Calm, Mental Clarity, and Sleep and Relaxation blends – or the Immune Function Support variety. *www.seelecttea.com*

AUSTRALIA

The Koala Tea Company: A range of 100% organically produced Australian teas. Contact them on: *www.koalatea.com.au*

The Tea Centre of Sydney: They offer over 170 varieties of tea which can be ordered on-line at *www.theteacentre.com.au*

NEW ZEALAND

Creative Energy web site offers Madura Tea – a range of 97% caffeine free and 100% tannic acid free teas, all available through on-line ordering at: *www.creativeenergy.co.nz*

Milks, Juices, Cordials and Sparkling Drinks

Organics Direct: They have brought together a dedicated team of growers, producers and support staff to supply, to your door, a wide range of organic drinks and ingredients. For a copy of their brochure ring (UK) 020 7622 3003 or fax them on 020 7622 4447. Alternatively, you can check out the product range available and order through their web site: *www.organicsdirect.co.uk*

Provamel: A wide range of soya milk and soya fruit drinks, which are readily available at most health food shops and supermarkets. Contact them for full information on the range available at *www.provamel.co.uk*

Soya Dream: Manufactured by Imagine Foods, check your local health food shop or delicatessen for the range of products available or contact them direct through their web site: *www.imaginefoods.com*

drink to your health

Equipment

Check your local department store, supermarket or kitchen shop for infusers, filters, strainers, teapots and a host of other tea-making accessories. Or check out the following web sites to order items on-line.

Venalicia: A range of fine teas, herbal infusions and equipment, which can be ordered via their web site: *www.venalicia.com*

Fortnum & Mason: Established in the early 1700s, this world-renowned shop, based in the heart of London, offers a selection of wonderful gifts, including teas, which can be ordered on-line. *www.fortnumandmason.co.uk*

Whittard of Chelsea: Visit one of the many high street shops of this well-established firm – or order your tea or equipment on-line through their web site at *www.whittard.com*

 # Bibliography

Prevention's New Foods for Healing. Selene Yeager and the Editors of *Prevention Health Books* (Rodale Press, Inc. 1998).

The PDR Family Guide to Natural Medicines and Healing Therapies (Three Rivers Press, 1999).

The Medical Advisor, The Complete Guide to Alternative and Conventional Treatments (Time-Life Books, 1997).

A Handbook of Natural Folk Remedies. Elena Oumano, Ph.D. (Avon Books, 1997).

The Natural Pharmacy. Skye Lininger, D.C., ed. (Prima Health, 1998).

Herbs of Choice. Varro E. Tyler, Ph.D. (Pharmaceutical Products Press, 1994).

The Complete Book of Ayurvedic Home Remedies. Vasant Lad, B.A.M.S., M.A.Sc. (Three Rivers Press, 1999).

The American Dietetic Association's Complete Food and Nutrition Guide. Roberta Larson Duyff, M.S., R.D., C.F.C.S. (Chronimed Publishing, 1996).

'Communicating Food for Health.' Carol M. Coughlin, R.D. (January 2000: p. 9).

'Boost Your Brainpower.' Ellen Michaud, Russ Wild and the Editors of *Prevention* magazine (Rodale Press, Inc. 1991).

'Topics in Nutrition, Women, Food, and Mood.' Mindy S. Kurzer, Ph.D. Hershey Foods Corporation (September 1996).

'What Is SAMe?' *Newsweek.* Geoffrey Cowley and Anne Underwood (July 5, 1999).

True Thai. Victor Sodsook, with Theresa Volpe Laursen and Byron Laursen (William Morrow and Company, 1995).

'Women Need to Beef Up Dietary Zinc.' *Tufts University Health & Nutrition Letter* (January 2000, vol. 17, No. 11: p. 1).

'Killing Bacteria — with Cinnamon?' *Tufts University Health & Nutrition Letter* (October 1999, vol. 17, no. 8: p. 2).

Baking Soda. Vicki Lansky (The Book Peddlers, Deephaven, Minnesota, 1995).

'Food Sources of Added Sweeteners in the Diets of Americans.' *Journal of the American Dietetic Association.* Joanne F. Guthrie, Ph.D., M.P.H., R.D.; Joan F. Morton, M.S. (January 2000, vol. 100, No. 1: pp. 43–48).

'Water: The Elixir of Life.' *Current Concepts and Perspectives in Nutrition.* Barbara Levine, Ph.D., R.D. (February 1999, vol. 9, No. 1: pp. 1–8).

Index

drink to your health

h

hangovers, 74, 128, 229
headaches, 69, 100, 103, 229–30
hearing loss, 230
heart disease, 31, 38, 46, 52, 55–6, 60,
    66, 78, 88, 129, 171, 179, 190,
    230–1
Heart Soothing Chai, 111–12
haemorrhoids, 65, 231–2
Hi-Pro, 48, 220, 223
High Po, 76, 232
High C, 29, 218, 222, 223
Homemade Beetroot Borscht, 149, 219,
    233
Homemade Ginger Ale, 132, 237
honey, 29, 81, 89–90, 99, 104, 106,
    111, 118, 126, 181, 183, 185, 200
honeydew melon, 61
Hot Garlic, Carrot, and Broccoli Soup,
    156–7, 222, 225, 236, 238
Hot Ginger Tea, 203
hypoglycaemia, 232–3

i

Iced Mochaccino, 100, 230
immune system, 24–5, 29, 36, 44, 69,
    74, 93–4, 104–5, 110, 120, 131,
    133, 139, 143, 145, 147, 156,
    166, 178, 192, 194, 212
indigestion, 182
infusions, 86
insomnia, 85, 107, 187, 233
irritable bowel syndrome, 64–5, 72,
    108, 234
Island Powerhouse, 70, 239
isoflavones, 190

j

jasmine tea, 104
Jewish Penicillin, 160–1, 224–5, 235

juices

Arthritis Relief, 23, 219
Cancer Phyter, 24, 222
Elizabeth's Healing Cocktail, 34,
    224, 239
Faux Café, 28, 226
Ginger Apricot Support, 31, 217,
    218, 231
Good Time Party Punch, 38, 221,
    223, 231
High-C, 29, 218, 222, 223
One-Two Punch, 33, 220
Piquant Pomegranate, 36, 219
Tutti Fruiti on the Rocks, 27, 226

k

kale, 156
kiwi, 72–4, 78
Kiwi Soya Smoothie, 73, 231
Kiwi Strawberry Smoothie, 74, 229,
    239

l

lactose-free milk, 64
Laursen, Byron, 113
Laursen, Theresa Volpe, 113
Leanne's Orange Passion, 139, 224
Lemon Aid, 126, 224
lemon balm, 106
Lemon Balm Anxiety Reducer, 85, 217,
    233–4, 239, 240
lemon balm tea, 85
lemon juice, 29, 76, 81, 89, 102,
    125–6, 149, 200, 205
lemongrass, 113
Lemongrass Ginger Tea, 113
Licorice Root Soother, 90–1, 225
licorice root tea, 90
lime juice, 76, 87, 127, 134
loss of appetite, 217
low blood sugar, 199

FOODS THAT FIGHT PAIN
by Neal Barnard, M.D.

'One of the most responsible and authoritative voices in American medicine today'
Andrew Weil, author of *Spontaneous Healing*

More and more people today are looking beyond conventional medicine in their search for good health. Now, in this remarkable and timely book, Dr Neal Barnard shows us how to soothe everyday ailments and cure a host of chronic pain conditions by using common foods, traditional supplements and herbs. For example, did you know that ginger can prevent migraines and that coffee sometimes cures them? Did you know that rice can calm your digestion, or that sugar can make you more sensitive to pain?

Drawing on new research by some of the most prestigious medical centres from around the world, Dr Barnard offers invaluable advice on which foods can contribute to pain, and how to avoid them, together with detailed information on pain-safe, nutritious foods that restore the body's natural balance.

Practical, comprehensive and complete with a range of delicious, easy-to-follow recipes, *Foods That Fight Pain* is a revolutionary nutritional approach to healing that has the power to transform your diet – and your life.

'One of the most practical and useful books you'll ever read. I highly recommend it'
Dean Ornish, M.D., author of *Dr Dean Ornish's Program for Reversing Heart Disease*

A Bantam Paperback
0 553 81237 8

A SELECTION OF NON-FICTION TITLES
AVAILABLE FROM BANTAM BOOKS

THE PRICES SHOWN BELOW WERE CORRECT AT THE TIME OF GOING TO PRESS. HOWEVER
TRANSWORLD PUBLISHERS RESERVE THE RIGHT TO SHOW NEW RETAIL PRICES ON COVERS
WHICH MAY DIFFER FROM THOSE PREVIOUSLY ADVERTISED IN THE TEXT OR ELSEWHERE.

50662 5	SIMPLE ABUNDANCE	*Sarah Ban Breathnach*	£12.99
81260 2	SOMETHING MORE	*Sarah Ban Breathnach*	£12.99
81237 8	FOODS THAT FIGHT PAIN	*Dr Neal Barnard*	£7.99
34539 7	HANDS OF LIGHT	*Barbara Ann Brennan*	£19.99
35456 6	LIGHT EMERGING	*Barbara Ann Brennan*	£19.99
81367 6	PERFECT HEALTH	*Deepak Chopra*	£12.99
17332 4	QUANTUM HEALING	*Deepak Chopra*	£12.99
81295 5	AWAKENING TO THE SACRED	*Lama Surya Das*	£8.99
81366 8	AWAKENING THE BUDDHIST HEART	*Lama Surya Das*	£8.99
40406 7	FIT FOR LIFE COOKBOOK	*Marilyn Diamond*	£8.99
17355 3	FIT FOR LIFE	*Harvey & Marilyn Diamond*	£8.99
81348 X	THE FALSE FAT DIET	*Elson Haas*	£7.99
81323 4	THE JOURNEY TO YOU	*Ross Heaven*	£7.99
81324 2	SPIRIT IN THE CITY	*Ross Heaven*	£7.99
50527 0	ANATOMY OF THE SPIRIT	*Caroline Myss*	£7.99
50712 5	WHY PEOPLE DON'T HEAL AND HOW THEY CAN		
		Caroline Myss	£7.99
81248 3	THE THERAPEUTIC GARDEN	*Donald Norfolk*	£7.99
50592 0	ANAM CARA	*John O'Donohue*	£7.99
81241 6	ETERNAL ECHOES	*John O'Donohue*	£7.99
81347 1	STAYING SANE	*Raj Persaud*	£7.99
40902 6	THE CELESTINE PROPHECY	*James Redfield*	£7.99
50638 2	THE SECRET OF SHAMBHALA	*James Redfield*	£7.99
81301 3	TAKE TIME FOR YOUR LIFE	*Cheryl Richardson*	£7.99
81371 4	LIFE MAKEOVERS	*Cheryl Richardson*	£7.99
17203 4	THE COMPLETE SCARSDALE DIET	*Herman Tarnower &*	
		Samm Sinclair Baker	£5.99
81380 3	SHAMAN, HEALER, SAGE	*Alberto Villoldo*	£7.99
40397 4	THE FRAGRANT PHARMACY	*Valerie Ann Worwood*	£8.99

All Transworld titles are available by post from:

Bookpost, PO Box 29, Douglas, Isle of Man, IM99 1BQ

Credit cards accepted. Please telephone 01624 836000,
fax 01624 837033, Internet http://www.bookpost.co.uk
or e-mail: bookshop@enterprise.net for details

Free postage and packing in the UK. Overseas customers:
allow £1 per book (paperbacks) and £3 per book (hardbacks)